# FIRST FRENCH
## *ESSAIS*

Venturing into
Writing, Marriage,
& France

# KRISTIN ESPINASSE

## FWD
Provence · France

For Jean-Marc, for teaching me
to live well and to love well.

And to our children, Max and Jackie,
who are wonderful examples.

Stories and photos copyright © 2014 Kristin Espinasse
*www.French-Word-A-Day.com*

All rights reserved.

Book design by TLC Graphics, *www.TLCGraphics.com*
Cover design by Tamara Dever, Interior Design: Erin Stark
Translation by Carol Donnay; translation edits by Alain Braux and Agnès Gros
Proofreading by Barb Munson, *www.MunsonCommunications.com*
and Kathy Tinoco
eBook conversion: Tom Dever
ISBN: 978-1-4961395-5-9

Near the great Mont Ventoux a vineyard
is carpeted by mustard flowers.

# ACKNOWLEDGMENTS

My deepest thanks go out to French Word-A-Day readers for your enthusiasm, encouragement, and support. More than reading these stories, you sent in corrections and suggestions—all the while offering cheers of *bonne continuation!* I set out to name every person who offered a comma or a grammar alert but this quickly proved to be a dashing pursuit—*with lots of dashing left and right trying to track down everybody.* To all these red penners, please know I am very grateful to you!

And *merci beaucoup* to Carol Donnay for proofreading this work in French—and catching several English peccadilloes along the way!

I would also like to thank Tamara Dever and Erin Stark—my book angels at TLC Graphics. Tami makes beautiful book covers and Erin's book interiors really polish a writer's work! Their sparkling touch reminds me of a tip I gleaned when struggling in school. While reading *Where There's A Will There's an A*, I learned the importance of good presentation: adding a nice cover to a report and using clear handwriting—these alone could raise a grade! My French hairdresser, years later, mirrored this tip. When running her hands through my lifeless hair, she'd snap her gum and say, "Honey, we're going to try to put all chance on your side!" *Chérie, on va essayer de mettre toutes les chances de ton côté!*

Finally, to my very dear family, thank you for encouraging me to write about many subjects, including my favorite: *you.*

# TABLE OF CONTENTS

An old blue *charrette*, or wagon,
near the town of Vidauban.

# VALORISANT
## (an introduction...)

**In 2003 I quit my secretarial job to chase my dream of writing.** Waving goodbye to my demanding supervisors, I owed them thanks all the same. The work had pushed me out of my sheltered nest and into France's lively workforce. I could now fly with my own wings, instead of depending so heavily on my husband, aka *Papa Poule*, or Father Hen.

From the moment I met him—while on a study abroad program—Jean-Marc took me under his wing. And when I had to return to America, to finish college, he called, he wrote, and he even sent telegrams! But it would be another year before he could invite me to share his Mediterranean perch. *And what a poetic invitation it was*, sent via a string of romantic letters culminating in a proposal: would I like to move back to France to live with him? *Would I!*

Our first years together were a little bumpier than expected, but now we were married and living in Les Arcs-sur-Argens, with two children under the age of 4. Here, a stone's throw from St. Tropez, my husband worked as Director of Sales at a prestigious vineyard. Though he was trained as an accountant, he had decided to follow his heart to wine country, where he would one day make his own gold-medal winners.

I watched the careers of our friends launch, too, and, nearing the age of 30, I still had not figured out where I belonged in the professional scheme of things. I wanted a passionate métier too, but what kind of job was I qualified for *as a French major*? It wasn't as though my area of expertise—language—gave me an advantage over job seekers here in France. I'd come to the pride-busting conclusion that all those A's I'd worked up to in Advanced French did not reflect reality. (Currently my toddler, Max, was coaching me on my pronunciation.)

One day Jean-Marc mentioned the cellar crew needed help bottling the wine. Did I want the job? It started tomorrow....

Having spent the previous years changing diapers, I began to question my ability to keep up with professionals. And what about communication? Since moving to France, I seemed to be using less and less of my French. With the birth of our son, I had returned to my native tongue. I knew it was important to teach my children English, but each time their father spoke to us in French I lost track of my efforts. The result was a kind of inbred language, wherein my husband ended my sentences *and my children began them*:

(Them): *Bonbons!*

(Me): *Bonbons?* Oh, *non...* no candy before dinner!

If juggling languages was a struggle, I'm even worse at multitasking. Weighing my husband's proposition, I pictured a lively production line, or *mise en bouteilles,* and saw myself breaking a lot of bottles as they swept past me and my reveries. At heart I was a dreamer, which amounted to an anti-skill when it came to fast-moving glass. Eventually, I chickened out on the opportunity and fell deeper into a well of self-doubt.

When Jean-Marc left his job at the vineyard, where we lived rent-free, it was time to push doubts aside and give up the luxury of questioning my value to the French economy. We needed another paycheck coming in, *tout de suite*! While at a social gathering for expats, I met a savvy business woman who knew of an opening. And that is how I landed the so-called secretarial job.

I quickly learned that the job was *un poste polyvalent.* I would be helping out in many areas (or, as a middle-age colleague complained, *Here they'll squeeze you like an orange! They'll get as much work out of you as they can!*). When my colleagues weren't sharing conspiratorial warnings, they were mumbling bitterly, *"Tout nouveau, tout beau!"*

(A new broom sweeps clean!) I gathered that meant the new hires (like myself) sparkled a little more in the eyes of supervisors. Though my colleagues were referring to favoritism, I soon discovered an ironic truth behind their words. I would indeed sparkle in the eyes of my supervisors. I just didn't realize that meant I would be handed a mop—with which to polish the floors....

My duties went beyond drafting letters. I helped out in the tasting room, pouring wine for tourists and professionals and cleaning out all the murky spittoons afterwards. I was also expected to set up our conference center, with pencils, notepads, and a bowl of candy for each participant (refilling the bowls after each break, I was amazed at how much candy executives ate!). Before the wine tastings and the conferences, I had to wash and clean the floors and the toilets, and was surprised to learn that business managers and directors did many of the things my toddlers did: threw toilet paper on the floor, splashed water all around the countertops, and sometimes they forgot to flush! I guessed they were in a rush and just didn't stop to consider.

When I was asked to give guided visits of the vineyard, I stole a few of those *bonbons* from one of the candy dishes and seized the chance to speak before a group of professionals. I panicked before that first tour and had to hurry back to the bathroom I had just cleaned for the tourists. I turned on the tap and drank handfuls, remembering the paper cups of water the school nurse once gave me to relax. I mopped my brow with a paper towel, before using it to dry the countertops. But my head was spinning. What if I passed out in front of the group? I had a bad track-record for public speaking, beginning in high-school geography class, where I blacked out before my peers.

I kept my balance during the guided tours and when the cook (another of my supervisors) asked me to keep an eye on the pots of rosemary... and the winemaker (another of my bosses) asked me to translate his poems, I wondered if garden duties and translation were being added to my responsibilities. And so I did what any American would do: I asked for a raise—and was quickly denied. (*This is an agricultural post*, my boss informed me. *And the salary is set.*)

One day, while doing inventory for the wine, I was told to find a solution to the spreadsheet problems we were having. Stress was put on the entire sales team (me and another "polyvalent worker"—this one a maid turned Marketing Director). We needed to solve a complex programming issue—one we had no clue how to handle. Day by day one of my superiors turned up the heat, until the atmosphere was boiling. *Solve the problem, or else!* He minced no words in a dire attempt to scare the maids-come-mathematicians into settling the accounts.

Sometime around then I overheard a word mumbled by my colleagues: *valorisant*. But what did it mean? *Ce n'est pas un travail valorisant.* It's thankless work, they seemed to be saying—work that didn't give you a sense of accomplishment.

*Valorisant*… the word grew, now beating inside of me until I began to sense a long-lost yearning. It finally occurred to me that rather than clean up someone else's mess, I'd rather clean up my own. *And rather than build another's inventory, I'd rather build my own!*

I thought about the blog I had begun months before. The online journal began as *un essai*, or attempt, at sharing my writing publicly. I called my site French Word-A-Day. After posting words and definitions for several weeks, I began a column called "A Day in a *French* Life." I soon discovered an added advantage to public journaling: by sharing my experiences with others, I could see life with fresh eyes. This change of perspective was *le déclic*, or turning point, in both my personal and professional life: frustrations became grist for the writing mill, and soon I was laughing at what once got me down. That menacing supervisor now looked very different to me and I could finally see the humor in the situation—of a "man of power" displacing his own responsibilities on the toilet cleaner. (Is that what my secretarial job had morphed into?)

From here on out I wanted to devote my energy to a meaningful pursuit—*une activité valorisante*. I realized that meant writing full time and not in the pockets of time surrounding work and family life.

With my husband's blessing, I quit my job and turned my attention to writing, learning to spell and to punctuate along the way. By working my writing 9-5, like a real job, I began to carve out the career of my dreams.

Eventually these efforts paid off when, out of the blue, one of the largest American publishing houses expressed interest in my stories! That stubborn intention—of selling my own "inventory"—was about to manifest! The book *Words in a French Life* was published by Simon and Schuster in 2006, and the story collection *Blossoming in Provence* followed.

Along the way I discovered a passion for photography. "Put up a picture with every post," Jean-Marc often said, while viewing my drafts. It seemed like a good idea, too—for if a story fell short, or rather, *left something to be desired*, there would always be a pretty picture to satisfy the reader!

May this selection of heart-written vignettes whet your appetite for France, and may you feel light on your feet when you leave the table.

*Je vous souhaite bonne lecture.* Wishing you happy reading.

*Amicalement,*

*Kristi*

Kristin Espinasse

*When Jean-Marc came to visit me in the States, after we first met, he brought presents— including this typical Provençal skirt. I ran to my room to try it on, but could barely get it over my hips. After more than a year apart, I think he remembered me a little differently than reality. This got me thinking about amour, and how we perceive one another. I squeezed myself into that skirt. I didn't see the symbolism then, but my next feat would be to fit into French life....*

*Les restanques*, or stone terraces,
in the town of Correns.

# MALENTENDU

noun, masculine
(ma-lahn-tahn-doo)

## MISUNDERSTANDING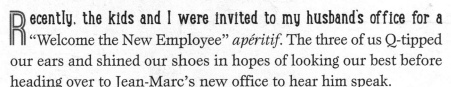

Recently, the kids and I were invited to my husband's office for a "Welcome the New Employee" *apéritif*. The three of us Q-tipped our ears and shined our shoes in hopes of looking our best before heading over to Jean-Marc's new office to hear him speak.

After the drinks, a few of the employees, the director, and the company's founder decided to dine at a nearby *auberge* in the village of Vidauban. When we were invited to join them, I signaled sharply to the kids—reminding us all to keep our act together!

At the inn's reception desk, we waited patiently for our table. To pass the time, the men smoked *clopes,* the children played a game of pool, and I maintained my new role of Delightful Wife.

Our act was running smoothly until one of us began rocking from foot to foot. No matter how hard I tried *I could not hold it any longer* and so tottered over to the reception desk to ask a pertinent question:

"Where is the *W.-C.* please?" I posed my question in French, trying hard to pronounce the unusual word for "restroom," which came tripping across my tongue and barreling out of my mouth as *"vay-say."*

"*Vaysay?*" the receptionist questioned. Confused, she turned to her colleague, who tried to translate.

"I think she wants *un whisky.*"

Shocked as much by the misunderstanding as by the indelicate manner in which the women spoke about me (as though I were invisible), I looked casually over my shoulder to assess any damage to our family's carefully constructed appearance. What a relief to find the director and the boss carrying on as if they hadn't heard a thing.

I returned my attention to the women behind the desk. "No! *Vay-say.* I would like… *une toilette*!" I whispered, hoping to shush them up, but it was too late.

"Madame wants *un whisky*!" the receptionist shouted to the *maître d'*, who stood across the room at the bar.

It took a couple of flapping arms to get my point across, before the *maître d'* offered a VIP escort—past the director and the boss and over to the restroom. Whether the company's top guns paid any notice I no longer cared, but was acting now on a more natural, no nonsense level. After all, when you gotta go, you gotta go! Or, as the French might say, *quand il faut y aller, il faut y aller!*

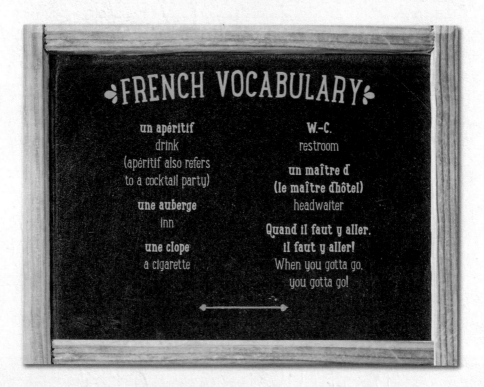

**❖FRENCH VOCABULARY❖**

**un apéritif**
drink
(apéritif also refers
to a cocktail party)

**une auberge**
inn

**une clope**
a cigarette

**W.-C.**
restroom

**un maître d'**
(le maître d'hôtel)
headwaiter

**Quand il faut y aller,
il faut y aller!**
When you gotta go,
you gotta go!

The painted fence reads: *Pour bien vivre,
bien aimer—et laisser dire.* (To live well,
love well—and let others say what they will.)

*Les volets bleu-gris.* Blue-gray shutters at my dear friend Tessa's house. The climbing vine is *une vigne vierge,* or Virginia creeper.

# TOILE

noun, feminine
(twal)

## CANVAS

Françoise has not changed much in the three years since Mom and I have frequented her art shop. She still has her ballerina-thin figure and still paints cherry-red streaks through her chocolate-brown hair; the contrast is as stark as her customers' paintings, or *toiles*, which line the store's entrance hall and make shoppers feel smug about their own art.

At the cash register, when I take out my *carte bancaire*, Françoise still picks up the phone to call over to the *papeterie*—shouting for them to bring back the hand-held credit-card processor (the one the two stores have always shared, never mind the inconvenience).

"*Moins vingt... moins vingt... moins vingt....*" Françoise mumbles as she tallies up the art supplies. She still gives my mom twenty percent off all items, and then rounds *down* the total. This morning she even threw in a freebie.

"Those paintbrushes have been discontinued," she said. "I can offer this one to your *maman*."

To this day, Françoise listens to my mom's English, only to reply in French. Just how the two women can understand each other is fine art to me. The paintings that result from their exchanges need not be translated either. They are, like the language barrier the women have overcome—or like love itself—transcendent.

After living with us for a year during which we helped her recover from surgery, Mom went home to Mexico. When she next returned to France for a visit, a few years later, Jules asked to visit her favorite art store. Driving back to Draguignan, we were shocked to discover that Françoise's shop had closed down. Standing out on the sidewalk, we stared sadly at the handwritten sign in the window; it read "A VENDRE." When our eyes caught on a bold and imposing reflection in the window, we turned to discover the bigger, fancier art store that had opened across the street....

Unlike Françoise's window, which displayed tubes of paint, brushes, and even a few modest creations of her customers, the competitor's windows were filled with a new rage: *le scrapbooking.* Ink pads, stamps, glue, and tiny cutouts crowded the window.

At the back of the glittery new store, a few paint supplies hung, like the end of a *belle époque.*

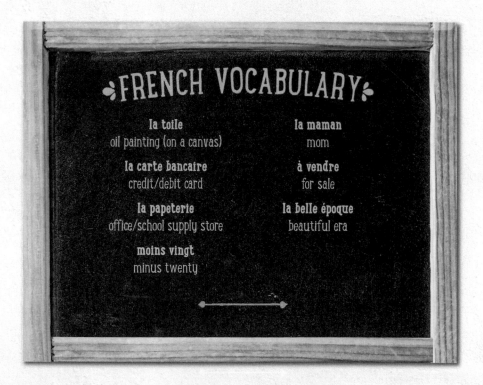

**⟡FRENCH VOCABULARY⟡**

**la toile**
oil painting (on a canvas)

**la maman**
mom

**la carte bancaire**
credit/debit card

**à vendre**
for sale

**la papeterie**
office/school supply store

**la belle époque**
beautiful era

**moins vingt**
minus twenty

*Une ardoise*, or chalkboard,
in the village of Suze-la-Rousse.
The University of Wine is located here.

*La vannerie* means "basketwork" or "basketry." This wicker shop is in Aix-en-Provence.

# PETIT SAC POUR EMPORTER LES RESTES

noun, masculine
(peuh-tee-sak-poor-ahm-por-tay-lay-rest)

## DOGGY BAG

One of the first cultural differences I encountered after moving to the land of bistros was this: *they don't do doggy bags in la France!*

In 1990, in Aix-en-Provence, a plate of egg rolls separated me from my future husband. Egg rolls in France are different from those in the States. In France, Asian restaurants serve the fried *rouleaux* with sprigs of mint and leaves of lettuce in which to roll them. *Les Nems*, as they are called, are Jean-Marc's and my favorite *entrée*, and we usually order so many that by the time the main course arrives we are too full to finish it.

At the end of that first shared meal in the *restaurant chinois*, we had leftovers. I explained to Jean-Marc that *les restes* in America go into doggy bags. Jean-Marc was amused by the term and his sensible side was quickly won over by the frugal concept. But when he tried out the idea on our waitress, asking her to box the food that remained on the serving platters, she showed neither amusement nor sensibility. In fact, she looked a bit put out by the request.

After Jean-Marc persisted, the waitress returned with an empty plastic tub which, according to the label, had once held pistachio ice cream. She pried open the container and slid the contents of both platters—and the side-dish—inside. I watched wide-eyed as the sweet-and-sour shrimp was poured right over the *canard laqué*, and the *riz cantonais* was heaped directly on top.

**Whimsical French penmanship on this hand-painted shop front.**

"*Ça ira?*" As the waitress scraped off the last grain of rice from the plates, her exaggerated gesture embarrassed me, cheapening an otherwise romantic evening.

Walking down Aix's winding cobblestone streets after the meal, I suggested to Jean-Marc that maybe it wasn't a good idea, after all, to ask restaurants to wrap up food. It was too awkward for everyone involved when the servers had to go scavenging for odd containers in order to be accommodating.

Jean-Marc disagreed. *It was a very good idea*, he assured me—*no more wasted food. The French would do well to adopt the practice of asking for a doggy bag!*

"But they are not doggy-bag equipped here, so there's no use trying to save the food!" As I argued my point, I walked right into a beggar. "*Oh, pardon. Pardon, Monsieur!*"

The homeless man, who sat on the ground beside another *SDF*, looked up.

"*Bonsoir, Monsieur*," Jean-Marc offered a warm greeting.

I watched my date, who smiled as he crouched to the ground, offering the homeless man the "useless" invention: *le doggy bag*.

The homeless man nodded in appreciation. After what seemed a very long pause, we said goodbye and walked on. Arm in arm, I pulled my boyfriend close. *This one was a keeper.*

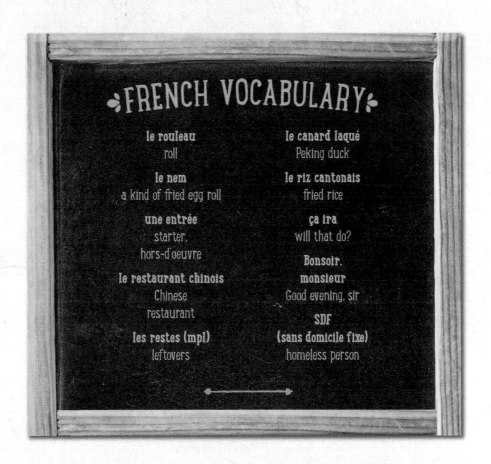

**❖FRENCH VOCABULARY❖**

| | |
|---|---|
| **le rouleau** | **le canard laqué** |
| roll | Peking duck |
| **le nem** | **le riz cantonais** |
| a kind of fried egg roll | fried rice |
| **une entrée** | **ça ira** |
| starter, | will that do? |
| hors-d'oeuvre | |
| | **Bonsoir,** |
| **le restaurant chinois** | **monsieur** |
| Chinese | Good evening, sir |
| restaurant | |
| | **SDF** |
| **les restes (mpl)** | **(sans domicile fixe)** |
| leftovers | homeless person |

*Les oeillets*, or carnations, and other flowers in the town of Figanières.

# FAIRE-PART

noun, masculine
(fer-par)

## AN ANNOUNCEMENT
(of birth or marriage or death)

This morning I received an email from a longtime reader. Only, on closer look, there was something unusual about the *courriel*: the sender's full name was repeated in the email's subject line. The last time that I received such a letter from a subscriber address it was bad news.

Clicking open the email, I soon learned that the sender was not a reader of my newsletter, but the son of a reader. The email was a *faire-part* announcing that his mother, Ginny, had passed away.

Ginny.... Like Cher, Madonna, Oprah, or Martha, it took only a *prénom* for me to recognize her each time her name popped into my inbox. I never hesitated opening her emails, which were full of warmth and self-deprecating humor.

Caught off guard, I clicked shut the email and sat back to stare at my inbox, where the letter was sandwiched in between dozens of emails labeled "SPAM." *Heartless spam!* I quickly deleted the intruder messages in order to safeguard this delicate *nouvelle*.

Clicking open the email once again, I noticed how the next line of the letter reflected the newly peeled sentiments inside of me, including sorrow.

The writer was apologetic about the delivery format of his message:

"I'd prefer a more personal way to let you know, but for many of you, this is the only contact information I have...."

I wanted to thank Ginny's son for informing this stranger, who, under the circumstances, felt something like a voyeur or an illegitimate mourner. After all, how to explain the relationship that I had with his mother, who was, in effect, a "virtual" acquaintance—someone I had never seen or spoken to before?

My mind was normally as busy as a hummingbird's wings, and now a new and sorrowful stillness reigned inside: a stranger's grief, my own.

I began to wonder. Had I answered Ginny's last email? I went back over the 61 *courriels* received from Ginny in the four-and-a-half years since she began responding to my internet column.

She addressed me as her "*Chère amie du courrier électronique.*" Other times, I was "*Chère Madame*" or "*Chère Kristin*" or, simply, "*Chère amie,*" to which she added, in her signature humble way "*si l'on ose dire*" ("if one might be so presumptuous as to say").

I noticed that self-effacing "P.S." that she usually added: "*Réponse Pas Nécessaire*" ("No Response Necessary," she always insisted, as if to say "you must, or should have other priorities than answering this silly note.")

In the dozens of to-the-point emails that Ginny sent, she rarely spoke of herself and, when she did, she mostly poked fun at her persona: "*Salut d'une vieille dame de Californie,*" she once wrote, and I can still remember the smile that it forged across this rigid-while-working face.

I learned that the "*vieille dame*" was a teacher, and "when lucky ... taught French." Mostly, Ginny offered encouragement and support. As to my first, practically pasted-together book (which she bought) she wrote: "I hope you sell a jillion of them!"

Whether in French or in English, her signature lines varied, and light-heartedly so, bringing to life one unforgettable character in my inbox: "Ginny '*la bavardeuse*'," or "Ginny in the foothills of the Sierra, off Highway 50." By associating a place with her name, I could better identify this French Word-A-Day *lectrice* in an inbox full of unfamiliar names. For me she was *"Ginny dans le Piédmont... where we are three inches low in rainfall,"* and "Ginny in Placerville, just downhill from Lake Tahoe," and, finally, *"Ginny en Californie... qui rêve d'un voyage en Norvège cet été."*

Ginny, wherever you are, in the Piedmont or, finally, up north (yes, "up north" I trust...)—YOU ARE MISSED. And while I never knew the color of your hair, the tone of your skin, or the twinkle in your eye—you were indeed a mystery to me—I knew a charming precious bit about *"la vieille dame de Californie."*

And one more thing, dear Ginny, I wish my own signature line had as much zip, character, and warmth as yours. I'm sure that the teacher in you would be encouraging—so here goes:

Love,
Kristin
*"une moitié-vieille dame de Provence qui a beaucoup apprécié votre éloquence électronique."*
("a half-old dame in Provence who very much appreciated your electronic eloquence.")

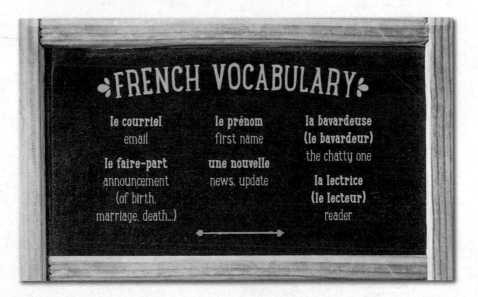

**⟡FRENCH VOCABULARY⟡**

**le courriel**
email

**le prénom**
first name

**la bavardeuse**
**(le bavardeur)**
the chatty one

**le faire-part**
announcement
(of birth,
marriage, death...)

**une nouvelle**
news, update

**la lectrice**
**(le lecteur)**
reader

The French love to call a line of pretty girls
*une brochette de filles*. Here's another line of pretty girls.
or *une brochette de chaises*. They were spotted in Bonifacio.
Corsica—where the southern French love to vacation.

# FRANGINE

noun, feminine
(frahn-zheen)

## SISTER ←⟿
(in informal French)

When Jean-Marc's sister comes to stay with us, the kids want to touch their aunt's pink hair, ride in her orange car, and give up their beds for her comfort. *Do you still live in a school bus and can we come visit?* they want to know.

The bus has been sold, she tells them, but there is plenty of room in her two-ton *camion*. The home being of a mobile nature, such a visit might be in Normandy or Paris or even Africa—wherever work or wonderment might take her. Aunt Cécile has worked as a mime, as a circus-tent technician and, most recently, as a driver for a punk-rock band—she even holds a *poids lourds* license.

Aunt Cécile with the pink hair drove up in an orange station wagon this weekend. She is taking the clunker to Africa. Her mission is to transport English books to a *bibliothèque* in Gambia. For cash, which she calls *flouze*, she will sell her car along the way, in Morocco perhaps, where station wagons are used as taxis. And while she is there, she—and the friends with whom she is traveling—will get the shots they need for Africa. Immunization, Cécile explains, is less expensive in Morocco. For the price of one French injection, she and her *potes* can each get vaccinated before venturing south along war-torn roads that lead to the destitute villages.

Along our manicured driveway, our family gathers for the *bon voyage* wishes. But before she goes, there are so many things I want to ask my sister-in-law about her life, one so different from mine.

"We don't ask these questions," my mother-in-law sighs, wanting to ask them more than I.

After my *belle-mère* kisses her daughter goodbye, it is my turn to say *au revoir*.

There we stand, side by side, my *frangine* and I—I with salon highlights in my hair, my sister-in-law with Mercurochrome streaks in hers (the dark red liquid stains it radical pink); I with diamonds on my finger, she with jewels in her soul. She is a French Robin Hood and her treasures are the cast-offs that she spirits away from the privileged. I am the stable, square, secure sister-in-law, still searching, longing to be spirited away with those old clothes and books of mine that are headed out the door, to Africa.

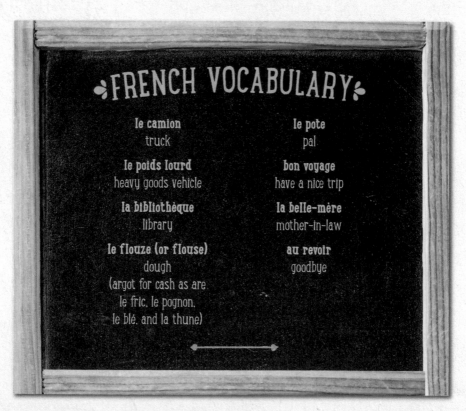

**⟡FRENCH VOCABULARY⟡**

**le camion**
truck

**le poids lourd**
heavy goods vehicle

**la bibliothèque**
library

**le flouze (or flouse)**
dough
(argot for cash as are
le fric, le pognon,
le blé, and la thune)

**le pote**
pal

**bon voyage**
have a nice trip

**la belle-mère**
mother-in-law

**au revoir**
goodbye

It's fun to play with words, especially when the effect
is harmonic: Baracavin = bar + cave + vin.

"Liberty, Equality, and Fraternity" is the motto of the French Revolution. Welcome to the town hall in La Motte.

# PÂQUES

noun, masculine
(pak)

## EASTER

I am lost when it comes to crafts and seasonal traditions. Still, it is only fair to share my American culture with my Francophone children during the holidays, despite an inherent aversion to dye, plastic tools, and, especially, instructions.

On the eve of *Pâques*, I search the kitchen for containers. I pull a salad bowl from the cabinet—*trop gros*. I take a soup bowl from the armoire—*pas assez profond*. I settle on an old wine glass, a jam jar, a mustard jar, a see-through coffee cup, and a tumbler.

As I organize the egg-coloring utensils, my daughter runs up to me. She is wearing a frilly dress with a black velvet *haut* and a white chiffon *bas*.

"You'll need to change if you want to help out!" I inform her. "*D'accord!*" Jackie agrees, spontaneously obedient.

I measure out ten tablespoons of *vinaigre balsamique*, annoyed when I can't find the 79 cent bottle of ordinary vinegar. Meantime, Jackie returns with her brother. Both children are wearing faded pajamas, the ones they are allowed to *salir*.

Max tosses the orange and the blue tablets—one into the wine glass and the other into the jam jar. Jackie plops down the yellow and the red *comprimés effervescents*, one into the coffee cup and the other into the mustard jar. Three sets of eyes dart to the remaining green tablet.

"That one's mine!" I declare, snapping up the effervescent disk and dropping it into the tumbler. The kids' enthusiasm is catching and for a moment I relax, set aside the step-by-step instructions, and tune in to the bubbly show before us.

We watch the tablets fizz in their *bains de teinture*. The colorful display livens up our kitchen. Next, we take turns emptying half a cup of *eau du robinet* into each glass.

"OK. Stir!" I say, and the kids each take a fork and whisk the water until the tablets are completely dissolved.

"*Allez!*" I say, bending the wire egg dropper (one egg dropper—two kids! Who put this egg-coloring kit together anyway?) and handing it to Max. Jackie and I watch with bated breath as Max lowers the cooked eggs into the dye.

"Careful!" I say.

After two successful dunks Max reaches for a third egg, but Jackie has a fit. Her patience has run out.

I understand my daughter's weakness, for it is just that—a lack of patience—that has kept me from beginning The Easter Egg Project sooner, and now *le jour J* is just around the corner! I estimate we are only about one-third of the way through our craft activity....

"OK. Now it's Jackie's turn!" I interject. "*Doucement*, Jackie..."

The eggs have settled at the bottom of the glasses. Time now to *laisser tremper* for thirty minutes. (Last year we followed the package instructions for "three minutes" and the eggs surfaced without color. The egg-dying kit is American-made, and it doesn't take into account brown-shelled eggs—the only kind we can get here in our French village.)

*Then there'll be decorating to do!* My enthusiasm ebbs as I stare at the messy tray and all of those tiny decorative stickers (I have a feeling they'll end up everywhere but on the eggshells!). I wish we could skip these next steps and have a cup of tea instead.

Just as I begin to get edgy, Jean-Marc pops into the kitchen and flashes an approving smile.

"It's so nice what you do," he says, as if I've always had this kind of patience. My husband's generous words touch me like a soft caress, until my cheeks turn the color of the *oeuf rouge*.

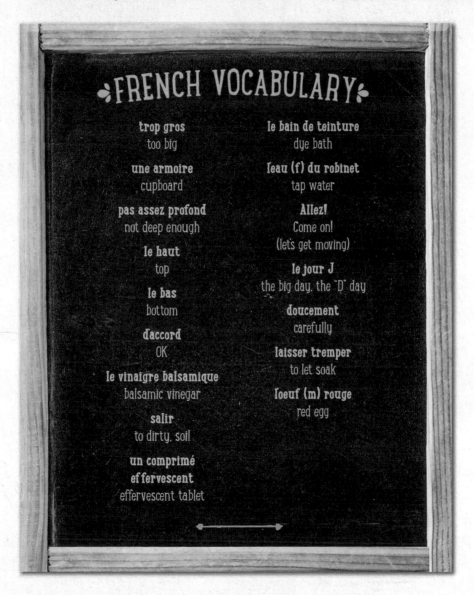

### ❧FRENCH VOCABULARY❧

**trop gros**
too big

**une armoire**
cupboard

**pas assez profond**
not deep enough

**le haut**
top

**le bas**
bottom

**d'accord**
OK

**le vinaigre balsamique**
balsamic vinegar

**salir**
to dirty, soil

**un comprimé effervescent**
effervescent tablet

**le bain de teinture**
dye bath

**l'eau (f) du robinet**
tap water

**Allez!**
Come on!
(let's get moving)

**le jour J**
the big day, the "D" day

**doucement**
carefully

**laisser tremper**
to let soak

**l'oeuf (m) rouge**
red egg

Our golden girl and rescue dog, Braise (pronounced BREZ). Here she is at her first *vendange*, or grape harvest, in Châteauneuf-du-Pape.

# POURSUIVRE

verb

(poor-sweevre)

## TO CHASE

At a café in the town of Camaret-sur-Aygues, we were seated beneath a shady *platane* when our luck took a swift turn for the worse.

Our five-month-old *chiot*, Braise, was sleeping beneath our table, her leash attached to the leg of a bistro chair. When our son rose from the same chair, announcing that he and his sister were off to play in the *vieux* village behind the café, our dog woke up.

Our golden retriever's ear trembled as she listened to the kids' voices trail off down the street. Curious, she shot up and set out to follow the children's laughter. But as she advanced, *so did the chair to which she was attached*!

The grating sound of the chair dragging against the stone path soon caught our pup's attention. Turning to discover the source of the noise, she was startled to find herself pursued by a screeching four-legged alien!

Braise's eyes shot open as she peeled out of that terrace café, the bistro chair flying off—bumpity-bump-bump—with her! The scene might have been comical if it hadn't been cloaked in what looked to be impending doom.

Braise swung left along *la grand-rue*, entering the town's ramparts, and continued full throttle down the pedestrian walkway. In vain, she fled the bouncing bistro chair, screaming bloody murder as only a dog can: in a gargle of excited barks. The commotion resonated throughout the town as Braise and the chair rocketed down the narrow street. Windows flew open as villagers poked their heads out of their homes to find out what the racket was about.

Terrorized by her screeching and bouncing pursuer, Braise tried to outrun the chair monster, but the faster she ran, the faster it followed, menacing and angry in her tracks.

In a panic, I chased after our puppy, screaming her name. When Braise was halfway down the street, the leash snapped and the chair fell away, spinning on its side to a full stop. Braise didn't look back but turned and headed, full steam, back to the terrace café *and to the busy street beside it!*

She ran right past me, rounding the next corner at record speed. And when she was just out of sight… I heard the screech of tires.

BRAISE!!! I screamed. *BRAISE...* With my heart in my throat I raced around the corner.

It was her tail that I saw first….

*Her lovely wagging tail!* Next I saw the sparkle in my husband's eyes—lucky stars of thanks that our dog had stopped just short of the oncoming car. Braise, *elle l'a échappé belle.*

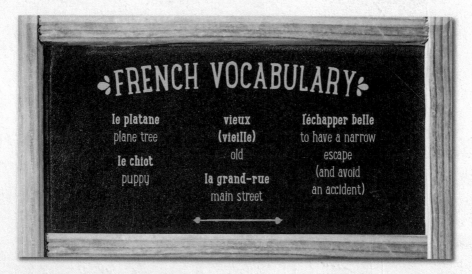

## ❖FRENCH VOCABULARY❖

**le platane**
plane tree

**le chiot**
puppy

**vieux (vieille)**
old

**la grand-rue**
main street

**l'échapper belle**
to have a narrow escape
(and avoid an accident)

Released from her cage at the pound,
Braise became Jackie's *meilleure amie*, or best
friend. Now life's scrapes and *chagrins* are nothing a
long walk (or skate) can't cure. Photo taken in Fréjus.

A winding *ruelle*, or "small rue,"
in the town on Nyons—France's olive capitol.

# BRILLER

verb
(bree-ay)

## TO SHINE

My mother-in-law and I are lounging on the back porch, sipping Coke and eating pistachios. We chat about *tout et rien*, while admiring so many wildflowers that have sprung up across the lawn.

Michèle-France has borrowed her son's T-shirt; the words on the front read "*Señor Frog's.*" Under the title, there are four caricatures—all *grenouilles*. Two of the frogs have on sunglasses, the other two, sun hats. All four frogs are wearing striped swim trunks. My *belle-mère's* pearl necklace is peeking out of the T-shirt; the combination of frog-T-shirt-with-pearl-accent makes an amusing, if unintended, fashion statement.

"*Il fait chaud ici,*" my *belle-mère* says, pinching her wool pants. "I don't know what to wear this time of year."

Sitting beside her, wearing a tank top and corduroys, I can relate. "*Moi non plus!*"

"*En avril, ne te découvre pas d'un fil ...*" my mother-in-law begins to recite a popular *dicton*.

I beat her to the finish: "*En mai fais ce qu'il te plaît!*"

As we laugh I catch a closer glimpse of my *belle-mère*. Michèle-France's fingernails are painted a glossy red. They are not too long, not too short: simply elegant. The string of gold beads around her

Not far from our back porch, the medieval village is blossoming.

wrist adds a delicate touch. My own nails are chipped and rugged. I would rather take a nap than paint them.

"Mothers don't always have time for *les petits soins*," my *belle-mère* sympathizes. Her words assure me she's no judge. She knows I am not lazy. Her eyes lock on the wildflowers as her thoughts take her back to her early days, to rearing three turbulent children. "Only one year apart in age! First Jean-Marc, then Cécile, then little Jacques." She shakes her head, tapping it comically for effect. Her exaggerated gestures are humorous but, like a clown's tears, they distract us from the suffering heart within. *I know she didn't cope as well as she would have liked to.* When will she forgive herself?

"Nice shoes..." she offers. Our thoughts drift back to the present.

"These old things?" I tease my mother-in-law, who laughs.

"Well I've had THESE for eons!" Michèle-France retorts.

I look down at her patent-leather loafers, as if seeing them for the first time. The familiar shoes, I realize, represent so much to me: a lifetime or two (my son's and daughter's), the duration of our *belle-mère/belle-fille* friendship, and the number of years that I've known my husband. They are that old. The dainty loafers with the chic square buckles have appeared at marriages and baptisms as well as funerals and hospital stays. I've seen them buffed, and I've seen them battered....

But today, *oh happy day*, how they shine!

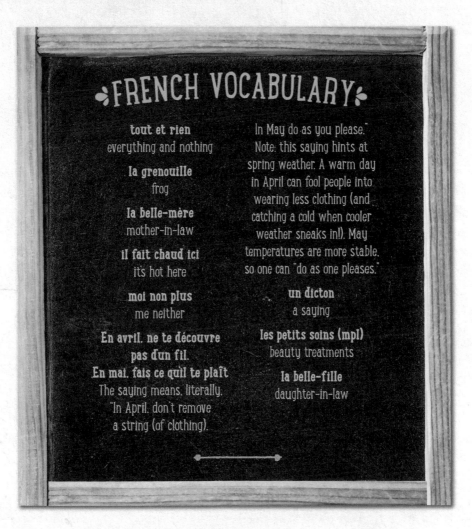

**✤FRENCH VOCABULARY✤**

**tout et rien**
everything and nothing

**la grenouille**
frog

**la belle-mère**
mother-in-law

**il fait chaud ici**
it's hot here

**moi non plus**
me neither

**En avril, ne te découvre pas d'un fil. En mai, fais ce qu'il te plaît**
The saying means, literally, "In April, don't remove a string (of clothing). In May do as you please." Note: this saying hints at spring weather. A warm day in April can fool people into wearing less clothing (and catching a cold when cooler weather sneaks in!). May temperatures are more stable, so one can "do as one pleases."

**un dicton**
a saying

**les petits soins (mpl)**
beauty treatments

**la belle-fille**
daughter-in-law

An old wooden shopfront, or *une vitrine*, in Cotignac, or "Pays de La Provence Verte" (Green Provence Country).

# AISSELLE

noun. feminine
(ay-sel)

## ARMPIT. UNDERARM

Jean-Marc's dear friend. Laurence. sits on the edge of Jackie's bed. Her long, wavy hair is pulled back into a clip, revealing her luminescent complexion, which is set off by dark Corsican eyes.

"*Coucou, ma puce*," she says to Jackie, who was sick throughout the night.

"*Ça ne va pas trop, n'est-ce pas?*" our guest coos. Jackie lights up from the extra mothering, while a light goes off in my own head: I should be cooing like Laurence! And it is about time I added "My Little Flea" to my own list of endearments for my daughter! Forget "sweetie pie"; *ma petite puce* is so much more... *French*!

"You might want to take her temperature," Laurence suggests, and I make for the medicine cabinet, as if I were already on my way to do just that.

*Le thermomètre*! Why hadn't I thought of it? Instead, I had pressed my cheek to my daughter's forehead, as my grandmother used to do, to judge whether Jackie had a temperature. Suddenly the old-fashioned gesture seems so clueless, so... *négligent!*

I return from the bathroom with a skinny glass thermometer *sans mercure*, one I picked up a few years ago after struggling to get the digital ear thermometer to work. Only one problem: where to insert it *while under the watchful eye of a seasoned French mother-nurse*?!

Do I do as the French—and aim for *les fesses*—or do I tuck it under the tongue as Mom used to do?

My daughter and her doting Corsican nurse are waiting. The room feels warm now and I wonder whether I, too, am coming down with something? A long hot moment passes before Laurence offers a suggestion:

*"Tu peux le mettre sous l'aisselle..."* she hints. I swiftly move the thermometer toward my daughter's armpit, as if I were on my way there anyway. Laurence nods graciously, as if she's certain I had been on my way there, too.

I am thankful for our friend's discretion and, in the end, for all the nursing tips I've just learned (including "add half a degree Celsius to an underarm reading"). But perhaps no one is as grateful as our little patient, who seems relieved that we aimed that thermometer at the armpit and not *les fesses*!

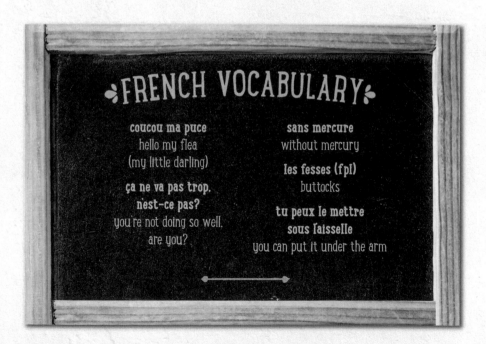

**❖FRENCH VOCABULARY❖**

**coucou ma puce**
hello my flea
(my little darling)

**ça ne va pas trop,
n'est-ce pas?**
you're not doing so well,
are you?

**sans mercure**
without mercury

**les fesses (fpl)**
buttocks

**tu peux le mettre
sous l'aisselle**
you can put it under the arm

In Brignoles: a colorful niche, shutters,
and shop front... We'll call this delightful
vignette *"Composition en Bleu."*

*Un cerisier*, or cherry tree, outside the town of Orange. Two *bagnoles*, or clunkers, rest forever beneath its branches.

# RAVISSANT

adjective

(rah-vee-sahn)

## LOVELY

At Michèle's home in Bagnols, I am waiting patiently to meet an Englishwoman who has lived through two world wars. It is easy to pass the time, seated here on a lovely terrace beneath the blossoming cherry tree. The picnic table is gradually filling up as Michèle's golden-haired daughters, Violet and Natalie, bring out roasted chicken, a lovely green bean salad, and baguettes fresh from the local bakery.

As the girls disappear into the kitchen in search of *les couverts*, the guest of honor arrives.

"I'm so sorry for the delay," she apologizes. "The workmen are busy cleaning my terrace. The tiles are covered with mold! I told the men to scrub it down with vinegar. *Vinegar works best!*"

"Hello Bobby!" Michèle welcomes her neighbor, *l'invitée d'honneur*. Bobby pauses to admire the cherry tree, which towers above her like a giant floral umbrella. I try to picture this delicate woman giving orders to a couple of burly *ouvriers*. In my mind's eye, I see the workmen reluctantly setting aside their industrial cleaners for the simple home remedy: *le vinaigre*—good ol' sour wine!

As Bobby settles into her chair, Michèle and her *belle-mère*, Shirley, shake their heads in appreciation of their friend's latest adventure.

"Oh, they must love you, Bobby!"

Bobby says that's possible, "Possibly because of the beer I give the men at the end of the workday!"

The ladies at the table laugh as Bobby explains what happens when she runs out of Kronenbourg.

"I knock on the neighbor's door…." We then learn about Bobby's 72-year-old friend. At 18 years her junior, *le voisin* wears a black toupee and a handlebar mustache, and provides back-up beer for the sour-scented workmen.

Listening to her colorful story, I notice Bobby's charm and how the flowering *cerisier* frames her beautifully. Its full, white blossoms muffle the rumbling of a thousand nectar-hungry bees. The buzzing causes us to look up through the trees, to the clear blue sky above.

"When the Mistral wind blows through, it chases away the clouds," Bobby notes. We search the *ciel bleu*. Not a cloud in sight.

The sky invites our wondering eyes and questioning hearts. I pull my chair closer to Bobby's.

"What brought you to France?" I ask.

Bobby tells me that when her husband died 12 years ago, she decided to come to the South of France and build a summer nest. She was 78 at the time.

As she shares her story, I can't help but admire her. Her eyes are that pretty shade between "steel" and "powder" that some call robin's-egg blue. Her short hair has that quality of white that tips the edges of the blue sea. I notice how it falls back off her face in endless waves.

Bobby is now talking about her 35-year-old granddaughter, an art teacher in Texas. As she speaks, I try to pinpoint her British accent. Just what part of *Angleterre* has rubbed off on her voice?

I notice her earrings: large pearl-colored disks. I make a note to wear such earrings in 53 years' time, as if *boucles d'oreille* would render me as beautiful as she.

Bobby tells me that her 63-year-old daughter has a butterfly tattoo on her hand. "She got it thirty years ago."

"Were you upset?"

"No. But I told her the butterfly might look different when her skin begins to wrinkle!"

"Does it?" I am curious.

Bobby eyes settle on her own hands as she considers the weathered *papillon*. "It is still beautiful after all," she says.

In the silence that follows my soul flutters from all that I have seen and heard.  I look down at bare hands as I search for words. I want to tell Bobby that *she* is like that butterfly.

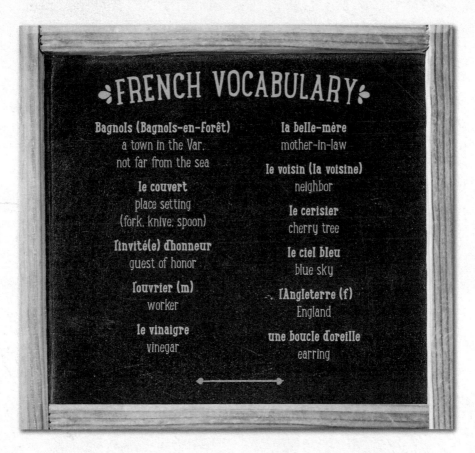

FRENCH VOCABULARY

**Bagnols (Bagnols-en-Forêt)**
a town in the Var,
not far from the sea

**le couvert**
place setting
(fork, knive, spoon)

**l'invité(e) d'honneur**
guest of honor

**l'ouvrier (m)**
worker

**le vinaigre**
vinegar

**la belle-mère**
mother-in-law

**le voisin (la voisine)**
neighbor

**le cerisier**
cherry tree

**le ciel bleu**
blue sky

**l'Angleterre (f)**
England

**une boucle d'oreille**
earring

*Une épicerie*, or grocer's shop,
in the town of Châteauneuf-du-Pape.

# EMPLETTE

noun, feminine
(om-plet)

## A PURCHASE

When Max and his *soeur cadette*, Jackie, offer to ride their bikes to the bakery, I request a little detour along the way. "Please stop by the *supérette*.

We're out of toilet paper!"

The kids wrinkle their noses, complaining that they'll look *carrément ridicule* shopping for *le papier toilette*. But, not wanting to lose the right to ride to town, they quickly come up with a compromise.

"Can we get *Sopalin* instead?"

I'm not crazy about the paper-towel idea, but have to give the kids credit for some creative problem-solving.

Half an hour later, brother and sister return from *les courses* with a few unexpected purchases. Jackie, her cheeks crimson from the cool autumn air, hands me a package of toilet paper.

"It smells like peaches!" she says. "*Sens-le!*"

I sniff the fruit-scented TP. It does smell good! Still, I am suspicious. How did she suddenly muster up the courage to be seen in the toilet-paper aisle? And what is that in the other bag?

As if on cue, Max pulls a bottle out of his *sac à dos*.

"*Du vin?*" Jean-Marc, walks into the room. He is as confused as I am.

"*Pour faire plaisir à Papa*," 11-year-old Max explains.

Jean-Marc examines the bottle, amazed at the coincidence: the *Côtes du Rhône* wine is from the area to which we will be moving this summer!

"It's a 2004," Max is busy talking wine with his dad. "It cost 6 euros 80 for the bottle!"

Busy reading the label, Jean-Marc seems unfazed by the fact that his child has managed to buy alcohol. More than fazed, I am dying to know a few details about the booze purchase.

"But Max," I question, 'How is it that the store clerk let you buy wine?"

"I told him it was for my dad."

My eyes shoot over to Jackie. *Eh bien!* That explains the toilet paper confidence. She must have told the clerk that the bathroom tissue was for her mom!

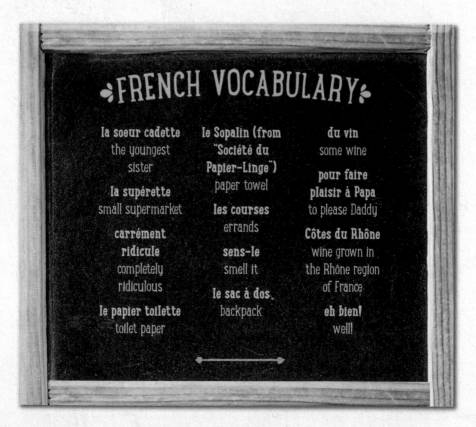

**❖FRENCH VOCABULARY❖**

**la soeur cadette**
the youngest sister

**la supérette**
small supermarket

**carrément ridicule**
completely ridiculous

**le papier toilette**
toilet paper

**le Sopalin (from "Société du Papier-Linge")**
paper towel

**les courses**
errands

**sens-le**
smell it

**le sac à dos**
backpack

**du vin**
some wine

**pour faire plaisir à Papa**
to please Daddy

**Côtes du Rhône**
wine grown in the Rhône region of France

**eh bien!**
well!

A candy shop in the riverside town
of Bourg-Saint-Andéol (Vaucluse).

Harvesting in Châteauneuf-du-Pape. You can just spot the château above my son's head. Behind Max Jackie and I harvest in the shadow of the crumbling castle.

# POURRITURE

noun, feminine
(poo-ree-tewr)

## ROTTING, ROT, DECAY

Of fourteen autumns shared with Jean-Marc, I have missed only a few of his uncle's grape harvests. Pregnancy and childbirth were two sneaky ways to escape the backbreaking *vendange*. But by the fourth family harvest laboring over vines won out over the other kind of laboring.

Harvesting grapes, like raising kids, gets easier from one year to the next. Perhaps it is due to age: old vines give less grapes; fewer grapes equal less work. As for kids: the older they get, the less lifting they require. On a purely physical level this all equates to less energy loss.

Harvesting might seem easier these days because of the language: with a growing French vocabulary I can now understand the *vendangeurs*, who are full of information—both serious and silly. All the trivia and teasing makes the time pass and before long the buckets are being stacked, the *sécateurs* stored away, and we're headed for Aunt Marie-Françoise's kitchen for a homemade harvest dinner.

Saturday afternoon I stood beneath a steel blue sky, my feet parked before yet another *pied de vigne*. Two rows over, my eleven-year-old was filling his bucket with clairette grapes while his nine-year-old sister collected the grenache further back. As for me, I held in my hand a bunch of rotten grapes.

"That's Noble rot!" another harvester, Eric, said, with a faux aristocratic accent.

I handed the bunch over to Uncle Jean-Claude who stuck his nose right into the rotten mass....

*"C'est de la pourriture noble.* We can use these grapes. But when the rotten grapes smell like vinegar, throw them out!"

I filed away the information before putting the nobly rotted grapes into my bucket and moving on to the next vine. When Eric's gray curls reappeared from the vines engulfing him, I noticed his grin was a little wider than before.

"Have you ever seen *les Baux de Provence*?" he asked. I smiled, realizing I had, in fact, seen the charming southern town in question. But before I could answer, Eric pointed to his innocent sidekick, Alain. *"C'est nous deux!"* It's us two! he chuckled. "We are *les beaux de Provence*!"

It took a minute before the play on words (*baux/beaux*) hit me, and a new translation of Eric's sentence registered: "Have you ever seen the "good-looking ones" of Provence? That's us!"

Laughing at his joke, I forgot about my tired arms, which were bitten and scratched, and my *reins*, which were aching.

When next I looked over to see how the kids were getting along I found them studying the grapes, trying to decide which were *pourri* and which were not. I marveled at the seriousness with which our kids carried out the task they had been assigned and I began to feel a little guilty about my own sneaky behavior of yesteryear (when I'd have done anything to get out of grape-picking!).

But I don't really regret missing the 95' and 97' harvests, which brought me two darling vintages—my very own "*Beaux de Provence*"—more precious than all the grapes in Châteauneuf-du-

Pape. Gathering my childrens' buckets, I tell them to head up the hill to Aunt Marie-Françoise's and Uncle Jean-Claude's.

"*Allez! A table!*" It's time for the festive harvest dinner, and time to celebrate family, too.

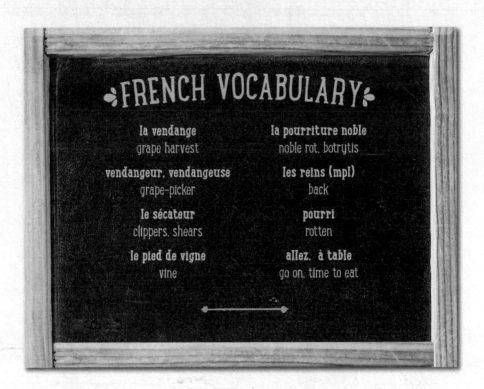

### ❧FRENCH VOCABULARY❧

| | |
|---|---|
| **la vendange** | **la pourriture noble** |
| grape harvest | noble rot. botrytis |
| **vendangeur. vendangeuse** | **les reins (mpl)** |
| grape-picker | back |
| **le sécateur** | **pourri** |
| clippers. shears | rotten |
| **le pied de vigne** | **allez. à table** |
| vine | go on. time to eat |

Jackie, approaching a hairpin turn,
or *un virage en épingle à cheveux*, as
she rides her bike in Les Arcs-sur-Argens.

# PLANER

verb

(plah-nay)

## TO GLIDE

With its winding cobblestone roads, our medieval village-in-the-sky doubles as a celestial bike ride for an 8-year-old girl. Standing on her bike's pedals, Jackie glides down the serpentine path of 10,000 hand-laid stones. Happy to walk, I follow behind my daughter and hear the intermittent screech of the *vélo's* brakes. She's a good rider and she is cautious when rounding those hairpin corners.

I'll bet the noise of screeching tires sounds like whinnying in Jackie's ears and that her imagination has taken flight—along with those wheels, which have turned to wings. Looking down, she no longer sees pedals *but the hooves of Pegasus*, the winged stallion!

For a magical moment, one little girl swoops over stones polished from nine centuries of shuffling feet, and glides alongside mosaic-tiled courtyards before touching down in front of our town's *campanile,* which announces the eighteenth hour in six resounding strikes.

My daughter's return to earth is jolting as only the transition from heaven to earth can be. With the lofty village at her back, she lands where the medieval district tapers out onto the modern sidewalk. There, she steps off her magical hoof-pedals and *right into a pile of dog-doo*. Just like that, her fantastical ride has come to a disenchanting end, no thanks to *les crottes de chien*.

"It's okay, Jackie!" I reassure her. "Everyone says it's good luck to step in dog poop! *Ça porte bonheur!*"

But my girl is inconsolable as she drags her shoe over a patch of *gravier*.

At first, I can't understand how stepping into dog-doo can hurt one's feelings so. Finally, I see the truth in my daughter's response. After all, isn't that how we feel when we fall off our high horse? We are vexed—our very feelings are hurt. We don't want anybody's sympathies! *Next, we sense the humiliation.*

I step aside and let my daughter sort through the you-know-what. When the pained expression leaves her face, she throws her right leg over the bike's frame and, with the push of the pedal (or hoof…), she's takes flight once again.

*Vas-y ma fille!* And never look back!

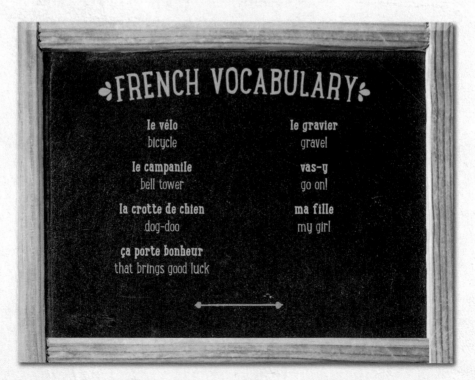

## FRENCH VOCABULARY

**le vélo**
bicycle

**le campanile**
bell tower

**la crotte de chien**
dog-doo

**ça porte bonheur**
that brings good luck

**le gravier**
gravel

**vas-y**
go on!

**ma fille**
my girl

In the Latin Quarter of Paris *un marchand de journaux* or newsdealer, moved into the Maison Queinec.

The old *kiosque*, or bandstand,
in Les Arcs-sur-Argens is located in the
parking lot in front of the *Maison de Presse*.

# PARIER

verb
(pah-ree-ay)

## TO BET

After driving around our town's parking lot and heading down the lane that runs between the old music kiosk and the town hall, we have come to the end of our possibilities. There are no available spaces. Even the illegal spots have been snapped up!

When Jean-Marc stops the car in the middle of the road, killing the engine, my nerves perk up and prepare to be rattled. *I know what he's up to...*"the Marseilles Minute"! And, knowing my husband, that rule-breaking "minute" will be bent to "minutes"! But there's no way I'm going sit here holding the car like I always do. Not this time!

"If someone comes," Jean-Marc says, "move the car."

At this point I am wondering if stopping for *bonbons* is really worth a parking *amende*.

"Why don't we just go straight to the beach," I reason, "as planned?"

"Because I promised the kids candy!"

We come to a compromise when I convince my husband to park in front of the *Crédit Agricole* instead. (A lot of people pull up there to use the bank's ATM.) Jean-Marc parks over the strip of yellow diagonal lines and gets out of the car. I watch as he crosses the

Bistro chairs are candy to my eyes!

street to the *Maison de Presse*, where the man who sells magazines and newspapers doubles as the candy man.

After waiting several minutes, Jackie wonders what's keeping her dad. "*Je parie qu'il regarde les journals,*" she bets.

"JourNAUX," Max pipes in, correcting his sister's grammar.

Five more minutes expire and we've swapped grammar games for people watching—waving to the villagers we know and ducking for cover when we want to avoid certain others. When the kids begin to wonder what is taking their father so long, I realize Jackie's got a point: *Papa* is scanning the sports headlines! Who knows when he'll complete his mission (he's supposed to be ordering "*deux mélanges.*" *Deux mélanges* are the magic words that cause the store clerk to fill two small *sachets* with a mix of candy from the plastic bins next to the register).

"*Je parie qu'il mange un de nos bonbons!*" Jackie bets, causing Max to zero in on the shop window and see if anyone is stealing HIS sack of candy.

Normally I'd be as alarmed as the kids, but this time I'm amused at the thought of Jean-Marc eating gummy bears in the *Maison de la Presse*. And he certainly isn't in a hurry—he's in vacation mode!

Finally Jean-Marc—in sunglasses and a Hawaiian shirt that reflect his casual attitude—returns. The kids verify that the candy *sachets* are intact and I look over to discover a third bag of sweets. *Qu'est-ce que c'est?*

"It's for you and me," the man in the aloha shirt smiles.

Mirroring his *sourire*, I pick up the small paper bag and notice the slogan next to the *confiseur's* name: *"C'est beau la vie!"* it reads.

The French words reflect my thoughts: Aw, yes! *Life is beautiful!*

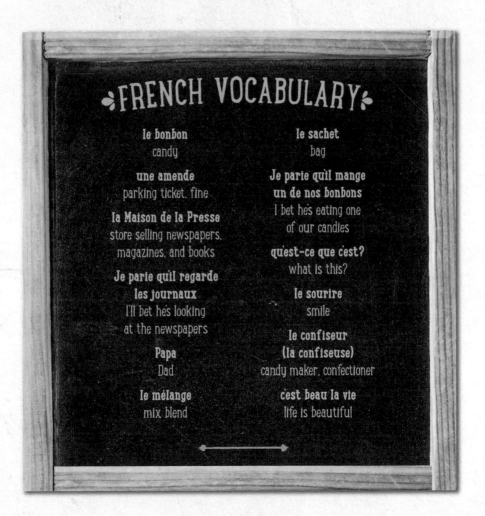

❖FRENCH VOCABULARY❖

**le bonbon**
candy

**une amende**
parking ticket, fine

**la Maison de la Presse**
store selling newspapers,
magazines, and books

**Je parie qu'il regarde
les journaux**
I'll bet he's looking
at the newspapers

**Papa**
Dad

**le mélange**
mix, blend

**le sachet**
bag

**Je parie qu'il mange
un de nos bonbons**
I bet he's eating one
of our candies

**qu'est-ce que c'est?**
what is this?

**le sourire**
smile

**le confiseur
(la confiseuse)**
candy maker, confectioner

**c'est beau la vie**
life is beautiful

*"Rentrer au bercail"* Do you know the expression?
It means "to come home." A furry friend on the
front porch and a pot of flowers are a wonderful
welcome home crew. Photo taken in Italy.
a favorite home away from home.

# CAFARD

noun, masculine
(ka-far)

## COCKROACH
(also: melancholy, blues)

Chocolate cake. It is one of the things that springs to mind when I think of my *belle-mère*. I see her cautiously stepping off the train. In her right hand there is a plastic Monoprix sack; in her left, a small overnight *valise*.

"*Attention!*" she warns, as I reach for her bags. "*Le gâteau...*" Knowing my mother-in-law, she's wrapped that cake with a few rounds of aluminum foil before balancing it on top of the few personal items in her carry-on. In the shopping bag she's got the latest editions of *Voici* and *Elle*, magazines she'll leave with me when she returns to Marseilles after her weekend stay. I know she's in good spirits when she is reading gossip and looking at fashion magazines, and when she's baking cake.

As for the chocolate cake, she's not sure if it will be any good. She's still building back her confidence after quitting cake completely, or the baking of cakes, that is. At one point in her life, making chocolate cake was akin to climbing Kilimanjaro: a seemingly impossible feat. That period, which Jean-Marc respectfully refers to as her "tired moment" was, truly, dark as the chocolate in her famous *gâteau* and minus a merciful dose of sweetness.

Chocolate cake and Max's smile: Rx for a grandmother's blues.

Around that time we were organizing a joint baptism/birthday party for our children. (Our eight-month-old daughter was to be christened and her brother would be celebrating his third birthday.) The food was going to be catered—all except for the dessert. Jean-Marc intended on asking his mom to make her chocolate cake.

Given my *belle-mère's* "tired moment," this seemed a cruel request. "Are you sure we can't order the cakes from one of the local bakers?" I tried to change Jean-Marc's mind, unaware of his sneaky plan.

"*Ne t'inquiète pas, chérie,*" Don't worry, dear. Jean-Marc assured me it would make his mother happy to bake the cakes. But I knew that was just his way of saying the activity would be good for her, a way to get her back into the bath of life. How symbolic the upcoming baptism was now, considering my mother-in-law's challenges.

When Michèle-France learned that her son had "ordered" three of her chocolate cakes—THREE!—she all but fled under her unmade bed. She had no proper cake pans, for one. For two, three, and four, well, let's just say that there began a scramble—a veritable scurry—to get the cakes together in one blues-busting hurry!

One week later the cakes made it across the French countryside, to the vineyard in Trets-en-Provence where the festivities had already begun. Jean-Marc greeted his mother, helping her out of my brother-in-law's car. I watched Jean-Marc pause to appreciate the cakes. Their undulating surface hinted at the transformative effort involved.

Later, I noticed Jean-Marc asking his friends if they had enjoyed his mother's chocolate cake. With each affirmative nod, I followed my husband's eyes over to his mother's and watched as he added an encouraging wink. My mother-in-law's face brightened time after time. Were those twinkles in her eyes?

"*Pour toi, maman.*" Jean-Marc handed his mother a slice of her own cake, thanking her for her effort. What had seemed like a "cruel" request, I realized now, had been a son's compassion in disguise.

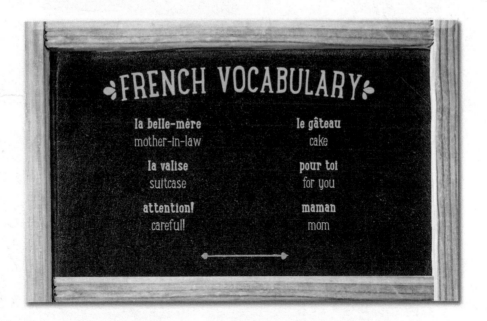

**❧FRENCH VOCABULARY❧**

| | |
|---|---|
| **la belle-mère** | **le gâteau** |
| mother-in-law | cake |
| **la valise** | **pour toi** |
| suitcase | for you |
| **attention!** | **maman** |
| careful! | mom |

Rocks on rooftops — one way the French keep their tiles
from flying off when the Mistral wind blows through!

# GOURDE

noun, feminine
(goord)

## FLASK, CANTEEN

*hope he finds his way to the bathroom at night,* I think, wrapping a piece of tape around my son's new *lampe de poche* before using a permanent marker to label it "ESPINASSE, Max." One of the first things I learned when I moved to France was that the French always capitalize last names; presently I could use a lesson on how to label dark socks....

I look at the navy blue *chaussettes* in one hand and my navy blue marker in the other. The dark socks will be difficult to mark, just like the flashlight and the gloves were. Too late to order iron- or sew-on labels. I remember the roll of tape.... Sure, it will come off in the wash... but then the packing instructions indicate that there will be no laundry service during the first week of summer camp. I stick a piece of labeled tape on the foot of each sock, happy to tick one more item off the list. *I just hope his feet will be warm enough.*

The light blue *bob* is easy to mark: ESPINASSE, Max (just under the bill), as is the tube of *crème solaire*. But will he think to put on his hat? Will he protect his little freckled nose with the sun block? And the back of his neck? The merciless Alpine sun now haunts me!

Max sits on the edge of the bed, twirling his *Equipe de France* soccer ball.

"Mom!" he protests, embarrassed to see me labeling even the little packets of Kleenex.

"But it says here to mark '*TOUTES les affaires*'," I explain, waving the list titled *Trousseau de base*. My son points a finger to his temple and taps it. A little *dingue*, he signals. His sparkling eyes and toothy smile soften my defense.

I open the smallest bag, and move the new orange toothbrush and the comb aside. I add a pack of tissues and zip up the tote. I hope he'll find relief up north from his allergies.

When I've labeled every sock, bottle, comb, tube, *gourde* and packet, I turn to my sparkly-eyed son. I feel like a dope marking so many non-precious items against loss, when all I really want returned from camp is this eleven-year-old boy.

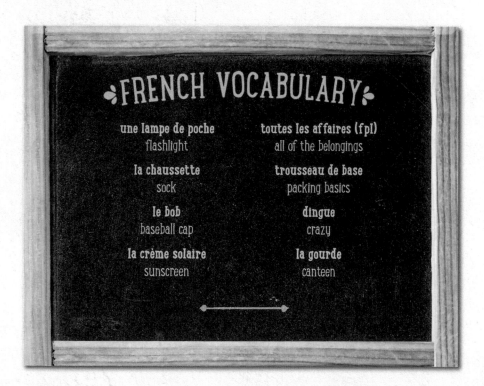

## FRENCH VOCABULARY

**une lampe de poche**
flashlight

**toutes les affaires (fpl)**
all of the belongings

**la chaussette**
sock

**trousseau de base**
packing basics

**le bob**
baseball cap

**dingue**
crazy

**la crème solaire**
sunscreen

**la gourde**
canteen

Sheets, undies, and tea towels—
or *les draps, les culottes, et les torchons*.

Come Christmas time in Provence you will see
*Le Père Noël* everywhere: climbing buildings like
spiderman... or "entering" a second-story window.

# INDIGNE

adjective

(an-dee(g)n)

## UNWORTHY OF. UNDESERVING

When my 9-year-old came running out to the garden. all teeth and waving an Advent calendar as if it were a winning *Loto* ticket, I had another of those *mère indigne* moments. Where had I stashed that one? I wondered, of the calendar.

"I found it in the bottom of the armoire," my daughter said, eyes still glued to the colorful package. Jackie didn't seem to mind that we'd missed opening so many of those little "doors" beneath the calendar dates, and I would soon understand why.

Still feeling guilty about the forgotten calendar (which I vaguely remember receiving in the mail a few years back, after it had been lost in transit) I set aside my book, sprang from the garden chair and its patch of winter sun, and followed my daughter into the kitchen to help put together the pop-up structure.

Because the assembly instructions were printed beneath the cardboard unit's base, I had to hold the 3-D calendar above my head and assemble it *n'importe comment*. (The added challenge was a good exercise in patience.) When all sides were taped, Jackie finished the Three Wise Men cut-outs and we taped their feet to the crooked foundation, beneath which twenty-four pieces of chocolate were hidden. Our project nearly finished, we stood gazing at a Nativity scene until the perforated "doors" caught our attention.

*La hotte du papa Noël.* Santa's sack.

With the help of Jackie's friend Manuella, we began "setting" the calendar to the correct date, a process involving the piercing of cardboard, the opening of numbered doors, the tearing of foil, and the gobbling up of chocolate.

As Jackie reached behind the door for December 1st, I noticed the dark candy was faded. When it was my turn to eat December 3rd, I discovered the chocolates were a bit tasteless and stale but that didn't stop me from eating December 6th and 9th. At this point the girls were popping open the doors and handing me my chocolates when I lagged behind the other candy gobblers in the race to set the date. It wasn't until I sat there with December 12th melting on my tongue that I realized I had forgotten something very important.

"*Quelle horreur*! I ate December 12!" The girls looked confused. "I mean I ate Granny's birthday!" (Now the girls looked amused.) "I mean… that means… *oh!*"

Panicked, I looked at Jackie, who was busy polishing off *The Day After Granny's Birthday*, a.k.a. December 13th. That meant it was too late to call Jean-Marc's mother on her *anniversaire*. I could now slap the label *belle-fille indigne* across my forehead.

Feeling worthless and dumb as the cardboard pop-up I'd just assembled, I dialed my *belle-mère* in Marseilles. As the phone rang, I looked over to the three cardboard Wise Men for encouragement. Two of them had already tumbled over from the faulty tape job I'd supervised earlier.

"We're not perfect either," they seemed to say.

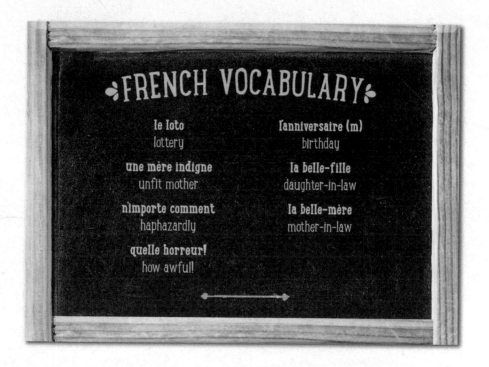

**⬧FRENCH VOCABULARY⬧**

| | |
|---|---|
| **le loto**<br>lottery | **l'anniversaire (m)**<br>birthday |
| **une mère indigne**<br>unfit mother | **la belle-fille**<br>daughter-in-law |
| **n'importe comment**<br>haphazardly | **la belle-mère**<br>mother-in-law |
| **quelle horreur!**<br>how awful! | |

A little *pêcher* and a newly-painted door warm the crumbling façade of an old farmhouse. *Un cadenas*, or padlock, discourages *cambrioleurs*, or burglars.

# PÊCHE

noun, feminine
(pesh)

PEACH ←🌀

## SCENE 1

My 8-year-old strides up in a leopard skirt, pink sequined sandals, and her swim top—the one with the real *coquilles* sewn on.

"*J'ai fait mon lit,*" she reports. She has also swept the floor of the *séjour* and, without my asking, she has watered the begonias, the tomato seedlings, and the thirsty peach tree. She must want something.

"*Je peux avoir une pêche, maman?*"

I look out the window to the fruit-laden *pêcher*—thirteen peaches this year! But shouldn't they be bigger than the fuzzy orange balls hanging from the branches?

"I think we should leave them," I decide. "They're not ripe yet."

"But it is the first day of summer!" my daughter pleads.

It is hard to resist her enthusiasm, all the more so when I think of the amusing scene I witnessed yesterday. Jackie was standing beneath the little tree, her nose pressed to a peach. She wasn't allowed to pick the fruit, but no one said she couldn't inhale it

## SCENE 2

It's four days later, and the peach tree is nearly bare!

"Who ate all the peaches?" I shout.

Max and Jackie point fingers at each other. Jackie swears she's eaten only two. As for Max, he's halfway to the front gate, about to take off down the street.

"You ate NINE peaches?" I scream, chasing after him.

"But most of them were on the ground already!" Max hollers back.

## SCENE 3

I am lying on the couch, a small peach cradled between my nose and upper lip. I don't dare eat it, but I can inhale it. Earlier, Jackie had tiptoed into the living room with the fuzzy peace offering. "*Tiens, maman,*" she said, sweetly.

The little peach is soft and warm, and the *chaleur* sends a strong fruity infusion into *chaque narine*, calming me and sending images of would-have-been delights: peaches 'n cream... peach pie... warm peach soup... peach cobbler....

The aromatic smorgasbord fills me up until I hardly miss the stolen fruit, but am filled with amusing memories of a couple adorable thieves and the stripping of a little tree, peach by peach.

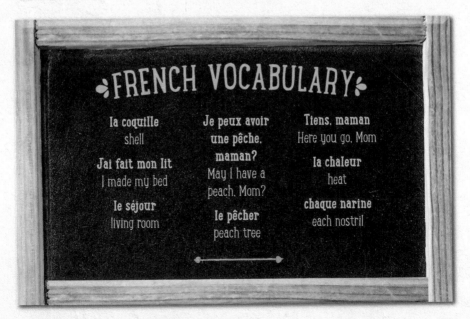

### ❧FRENCH VOCABULARY❧

**la coquille**
shell

**J'ai fait mon lit**
I made my bed

**le séjour**
living room

**Je peux avoir une pêche, maman?**
May I have a peach, Mom?

**le pêcher**
peach tree

**Tiens, maman**
Here you go, Mom

**la chaleur**
heat

**chaque narine**
each nostril

Sea blue walls and a beautifully crafted zinc
bar at the popular *Bar de la Marine*, where
Marcel Pagnol's *Marseilles trilogy* was filmed.

*L'embarras de choix* means, literally,
"an embarrassing variety of choices."

# LUNETTES

noun, feminine, plural
(lew-net)

## GLASSES, SPECTACLES

H and in hand my daughter and I stroll through our village. When we pass in front of the *magasin de lunettes* I slow, turn briefly toward the shop, and wave timidly. Almost as soon as my hand reaches up I quickly tug it back down again.

"Who is that?" Jackie asks.

"A friend...."

Originally, *lunette* meant "little moon." The word is commonly used in French for objects with a crescent shape, such as eyeglasses, and even toilet seats.

Last week I stopped into the *lunetterie* to get my shades or "little moons" adjusted. I noticed the shop assistant was in the back of the store. She smiled, pointed to the telephone at her ear, and said, "*J'arrive!* I'll be right there!"

I nodded *pas de souci*. She needn't worry about serving me right away. After all, I might not be a paying customer.

The fact that I might not pay made me a little uncomfortable. So much so that for two years I'd put up with sunglasses tumbling down my face or hanging lopsided on my nose. And the lenses, which are *de vue*, had long ago popped out. How many times had I retrieved *les verres* from the sidewalk, only to wrestle them back in again? These same lenses now sat unevenly in the frame's sockets.

Just like back home, in America, eyeglass boutiques in France do not seem to charge to adjust frames. So I always feel uneasy as the shop assistant puts his or her work aside to tend to my crooked or stretched out glasses. But this time I solved the dilemma by bringing along a *pourboire*. (I had tucked five euros into my pocket before heading for the optical shop.)

When the boutique assistant put down the phone and said, "*À vous, madame*," I showed her my glasses, apologizing for their tattered *état*. Next, I watched her push and mold the frame back into shape.

"*Essayez-les*," she said now and again, after sweeping the frames through hot sand. When the glasses were finally adjusted and snug against my face, I promised I would never again push them back as a makeshift hair band (this explained their demise time after time).

Next, the dreaded question: "*Combien je vous dois?*" And the predictable reply: "*Rien.*"

I smiled knowingly and handed the shop assistant five euros.

"*Non. Rien!*" she insisted.

I thanked her and looked around nervously. Seeing the optical shop also sold post cards, I casually mentioned I would need a few. In a haphazard fashion, I pulled together a half-dozen *cartes postales*, trying to get the sum to add up to five euros.

The shop assistant counted the cards and said, "*Trois euros soixante, s'il vous plaît.*" I handed her the five euro note and told her to please keep the change.

"*Non*," she insisted, handing me the coins. Next, she looked me directly in the eyes and said firmly:

"*Les bons comptes font les bons amis.*" Good accounts make good friends.

Now that the air was cleared, I no longer felt indebted. This time it was easy for me to walk away, as simple as saying *à bientôt* to a friend.

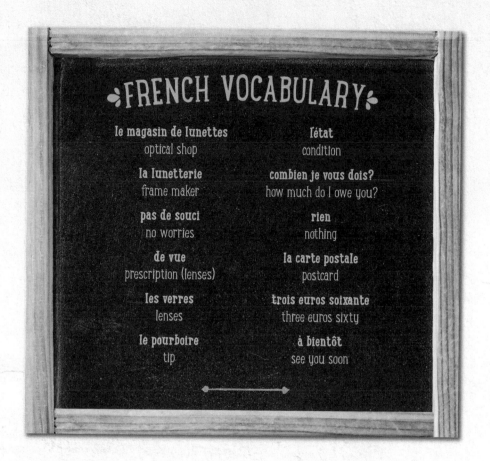

**❧FRENCH VOCABULARY❧**

**le magasin de lunettes**
optical shop

**la lunetterie**
frame maker

**pas de souci**
no worries

**de vue**
prescription (lenses)

**les verres**
lenses

**le pourboire**
tip

**l'état**
condition

**combien je vous dois?**
how much do I owe you?

**rien**
nothing

**la carte postale**
postcard

**trois euros soixante**
three euros sixty

**à bientôt**
see you soon

A Polaroid of Jean-Marc and me,
when we first moved in together,
in Marseilles. We are eating at *La Cloche
à Fromages*, or "The Cheese Cover."

# BOUDER

verb
(boo-day)

## TO POUT OR SULK

I notice my husband is shaving this morning, something he rarely does anymore, now that he's working from home as a wine sales rep.

"Where are you going?" I ask.

"*En tournée.*"

"Prospecting? Where?" I wonder.

"In Saint-Raphaël."

Saint-Raphaël? My mind fills with visions of the foamy sea, sandy beaches, sidewalk cafés and brasseries, the boardwalk, the boutiques, the *marché*, and the glamorous *Belle Époque* architecture.... Suddenly a *pulsion* comes over me. The *pulsion* to pout.

"I didn't know you were going out today...."

"Well, do you want to come with me?" Jean-Marc offers.

"You know I can't come with you. I have work to do!" With a huff and a puff I leave the room.

❦

In 1994 the only *conseil* Jean-Marc's ailing grandmother gave me before I married her grandson was this: "*ne boude pas.*" Don't pout when love gets tough. "*C'est terrible—insupportable!—une femme ou un mari qui boude!*"

I hurried to look up the word *bouder* just as soon as I returned from *Grand-mère*'s modest apartment in Lyon to Jean-Marc's studio in Marseilles. I was hesitant to ask my husband-to-be what the word meant. What was it that was so terrible, so insufferable… something a husband or wife should never ever do? And why had Jean-Marc's grandmother selected this bit of counsel above the rest?

"Germaine," as Jean-Marc's *mamie* was called, was a stern woman who saw the collapse of a family fortune. In Morocco, after the war, she peddled house linens from her Estafette (a converted military supply vehicle) as there were six mouths to feed. When her husband, a prisoner of war, returned from *la guerre*, Germaine continued to "wear the pants," selling her linens *porte-à-porte*, while her husband went seaside to cast out horrific battle images along with his fishing line.

My first encounter with Germaine had me watching the once-authoritarian-now-frail woman eat the eyes right out of the fish on her plate. No sooner had I recovered from the fact that the French serve their seafood with its heads and tails intact, than I witnessed this unforgettable eye-popping scene!

Apart from Germaine's advice not to sulk, she taught me where all those forks, knives, and *cuillères* belong on the French table, at once thoughtful about her bourgeois upbringing—and *méprisante* of it.

The French word *bouder*, it turns out, means "to pout. From *bouder* comes the noun *boudoir*, which originally meant "a place in which to sulk." Though the dictionary says that a *boudoir* is "*un petit salon de dame*," it is really nothing more fancy or exciting than a pouting room.

I return to my sulking place, and continue to work and to sniff. *Je boude, je boude!*

"We'll leave in 10 minutes?" my husband suggests, popping his head in from the hall.

"I didn't say I was going with you!" I snap.

"Well, if you change your mind, I am leaving in 10 minutes."

I continue to *faire la tête*, or "be in the sulks," while my husband prepares for his surely glamorous *tournée* along the French Riviera.

At my desk, I peck at the faded keyboard, staring into the dismal screen. I can't concentrate on writing a story when I'm so busy obsessing about my husband's freedom:

"Monsieur Espinasse goes to the sunny Riviera," I grumble. "Monsieur Espinasse would like the *plat du jour*. Would Monsieur fancy a glass of champagne with his *foie gras*?"

Despite my ridiculous imaginings and the cynical commentary that accompanies them, I know that reality is quite different. My husband's door-to-door sales day will be spent lugging 18-*kilo* boxes of wine from one *cave* to another, navigating medieval roads, trying to find parking in a small French village full of one-way streets.

The glamorous day will continue as he stops for lunch at a grimy roadside gas station where he'll pick up one of those preservative-rich sandwiches: *un jambon-beurre* or *un pan-bagnat*. He'll wash that down with a cup of bitter coffee before rushing to the next appointment. Finally he will weave in and out of traffic on the *autoroute*, struggling to get back to our village in time to pick up our son from basketball at the end of the day.

Meantime I will be working freely at my computer, trying to write the next great American story (or so my imagination would like to think!). To my left, there'll be a *café au lait*; before me, the adventure of my choice, if I will but find the words to transport me there. *Will I ever find the words?* Oh, to be transported!

"Do you know what the word *boudoir* means?" I am out of breath, catching up to my husband, who is loading cases of wine into the trunk.

"*Comment?*" What's that? he asks.

"*Boudoir*. It's French," I say.

"No. I don't know that word. What does it mean?" Jean-Marc asks, opening the car door for me.

"A sulking place," I laugh. "It's a place to *bouder*, or to be in the sulks."

"Are you in the sulks?" Jean-Marc teases.

"Oh no, not I!" I glance out of the car window, to the heavens above. I hope Germaine is watching. God rest her courageous, peddler's soul.

I look over to the other peddler, seated beside me. Germaine would be so proud of her grandson, who has, in his own way, followed in her steps.

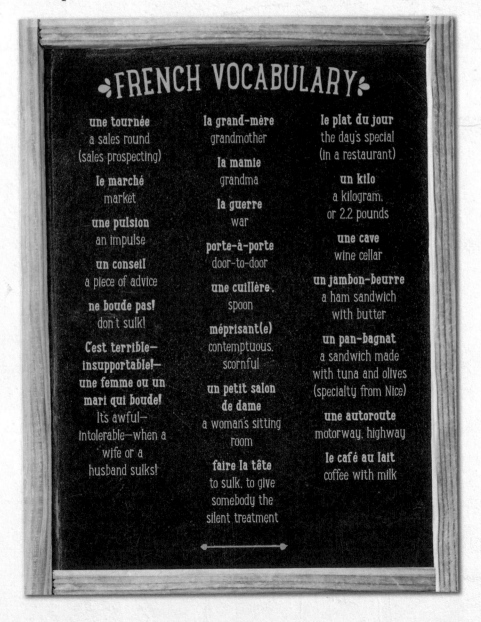

**❧ FRENCH VOCABULARY ❧**

**une tournée**
a sales round
(sales prospecting)

**le marché**
market

**une pulsion**
an impulse

**un conseil**
a piece of advice

**ne boude pas!**
don't sulk!

**C'est terrible—
insupportable!—
une femme ou un
mari qui boude!**
It's awful—
intolerable—when a
wife or a
husband sulks!

**la grand-mère**
grandmother

**la mamie**
grandma

**la guerre**
war

**porte-à-porte**
door-to-door

**une cuillère,**
spoon

**méprisant(e)**
contemptuous,
scornful

**un petit salon
de dame**
a woman's sitting
room

**faire la tête**
to sulk, to give
somebody the
silent treatment

**le plat du jour**
the day's special
(in a restaurant)

**un kilo**
a kilogram,
or 2.2 pounds

**une cave**
wine cellar

**un jambon-beurre**
a ham sandwich
with butter

**un pan-bagnat**
a sandwich made
with tuna and olives
(specialty from Nice)

**une autoroute**
motorway, highway

**le café au lait**
coffee with milk

*Le fer à cheval.* Next time you stroll through a French village and see a door with a horseshoe, notice the orientation! Someone needs to have a word with the French... before all the luck runs out!

You see a lot of *pins parasols*, or umbrella pines,
on the southern coast of France. And here,
some ruins in the coastal town of Saint-Raphaël.

# CHOC

noun, masculine
(shok)

## IMPACT, CRASH, BUMP

"*C'était tout bête,*" as the French say. It was so stupid, the accident I had at the end of my street. I had pulled up to the crooked T-intersection, slowing my car to a complete stop. Having looked left, then right, then left again, I pulled forward to turn, as I've done hundreds of times before.

*Crash!* I felt the impact before I even saw the car. I was well into my left turn when the right front-end of my car collided with the left side of the oncoming car. It was a soft *choc*—like a bumper-car bump, nothing abrupt (no slammed brakes, no flying glass or screeching metal).

There in the quiet French countryside, a stream of English words screeched across my stupefied mind. Hit! Neighbor? Mercedes… *Insurance*.

The victim, or *accidentée*, was indeed my neighbor. She pulled her black Mercedes to the side of the road, just next to the old, slouching mulberry tree, across from a field of hibernating vines. I followed, parking my car behind hers. The neighbor got out of the driver's side. Her daughter got out of the passenger's side. I got out of my car and met them halfway.

I asked if they were okay and assured them I was *navrée*, terribly, terribly sorry. They said they were fine, but the car was damaged. The three of us studied the shallow dent along the back door.

The next day I drove at a snail's pace down my street, stopping at the crooked T-intersection after putting on my turn-signal three houses back. I looked left, right, left, RIGHT feeling more like a wide-eyed deer about to cross a firing range than a "bonus" driver with 20 years experience beneath her belt.

A few blocks later, I pulled into the victim's driveway, afraid I would flatten the rosemary bush or crush a garden lamp or drive right into the swimming pool!

I rang the *sonnette*, fidgeting with my insurance papers as I waited by the door.

"*Entrez.*" I recognized the woman from the driver's seat. Stepping into the foyer, I noticed her laundry—socks, undershirts, tea towels—drying on an indoor *étendoir* just behind the couch, which held stacks of neatly folded clothes. The tile floor invited bare feet on its gleaming surface. Framed portraits of three smiling adolescents lined the hall.

As I followed the woman through the living room to the kitchen table—stopping when she stopped to flip off the T.V. and *Les Feux de l'Amour*—I sensed she was missing the end of her soap opera (the mouth-dropping, what-will-the-heroine-(or hero)-say-next cliffhanger part), all because of my moment of inattention the day before.

I followed my neighbor to the kitchen table, where she sat down. She wore a thin painted black line beneath each eye, and her short, auburn hair was combed stiffly back. I thought about how many times I'd crossed her on the one-lane country road. I always edged over, letting her pass. She never smiled back.

Why did I have to hit *her*? Why couldn't it have been the friendly hippie in the beat-up truck? Or the shy, retired couple—he who always nods in appreciation and she who enthusiastically waves *merci*? Why her?

At the kitchen table I notice the victim's insurance paperwork is complete. I spread out my papers and begin skimming the French paragraphs: Insurance company name; Address; Client number; Nature of accident... I hesitate before each blank space, mouthing the words to the questions.

"My husband usually does our paperwork," I say, only to regret the admission. I sound like one of those over-dependent housewives.

"I put this down for that one," the woman says, showing me how she filled out her own form.

"*Oh, merci!*" I say, copying as many of her answers as I can get away with, minus insurance numbers and addresses.

"My daughter speaks English," she offers suddenly, wandering off the subject.

"Oh, really?" I look up, noticing how her face has softened. "Does she baby-sit?"

"She loves to!"

Soon we are exchanging phone numbers, with a promise to call if the other needs help. Funny how awkward situations can suddenly take a turn, or how bad turns can turn into something good—like the chance to get to know your neighbor (and score a new babysitter in the process!).

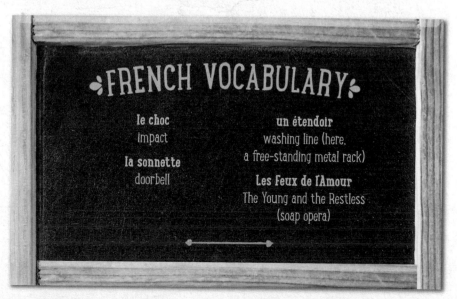

**❖FRENCH VOCABULARY❖**

**le choc**
impact

**la sonnette**
doorbell

**un étendoir**
washing line (here,
a free-standing metal rack)

**Les Feux de l'Amour**
The Young and the Restless
(soap opera)

*Le sacoche*, or bag, reads
"Room and board at Marie's place."

# MARRANT

adjective

(mar-ahn)

## FUNNY ←

When my friend Kirsten and her daughter, Morgan, came to visit, we huddle together on the guest bed to unpack while catching up on the good old days, or *les bons vieux jours*.

"How did we ever get our hair that big?" Kirsten muses, as we flip through some photos, remembering the 80's in Phoenix, Arizona.

I shake my head in appreciation of our efforts to glam up at 17- and 18- and 19-years-old—before we lost touch of each other for several years.

"Aqua Net!" Kirsten blurts out, answering her own question. I notice my friend's long chestnut-brown hair and how the sides are now swept back, smooth and flat, into a *nacrée* barrette.

I watch as she unpacks her bags, organizing her daughter's diapers and toys before hooking up a portable computer. Next, Kirsten unzips her carry-on and waves a red, white, and blue paperback through the air. "I'm going to find my inner French girl while I'm here!" she says, quoting from the book's title.

Kirsten's enthusiasm is contagious and I snatch the *livre* out of her hands. As I flip through the book, my friend recounts her experiences since arriving at the *Gare du Nord* in Paris, where she found herself waiting in a block-long line for a taxi. As she held her two-and-a-half year old, she was surprised by a Frenchman

Clotheslines in France range from works of art to comedy shows.
This one was spotted in the town of Nyons. I wonder whether my friend
Kirsten's been here and *pinned the yellow polo*...

who walked up to her and spoke. "You have a small child," he said. "This line does not apply to you!" With that she was spirited to the front of the *queue* and ushered into a taxi.

The stories of courtesy continue. "When Morgan fell sick in Paris, I called the front desk and a doctor appeared at my hotel room within an hour!" And while buying *pain au chocolat* at the *boulangerie*, Kirsten was touched to see a venerable Frenchman walk in, open a cloth bag one yard long and receive, as if on cue, the baker's baguette.

"I love this culture!" Kirsten says. "Don't you?"

When it comes time to tidy up, Kirsten is as courteous as the French in her quest to pitch in with the chores. She is independent—and she's even taken the initiative to hang out my laundry. I love the extra help!

That is, until I collect the dried clothing *and discover the protruding pin marks across the front of my shirts...*

On a positive note, the laundry is hanging inside out (this protects it from the sun's fading rays). But I cringe at seeing how the clothespins have been tacked on, over the fabric. Examining one of my *chemises*, I'm alarmed to see how the front juts out *here* and *there*—in the most unseemly places....

Shaking out another shirt, I check the front only to find more clip marks (and not at the waist line—but right across *la poitrine*!). Either Kirsten's inner French girl is being racy... or my friend is up to another one of her practical jokes again.

*Ah, les bons vieux jours!*

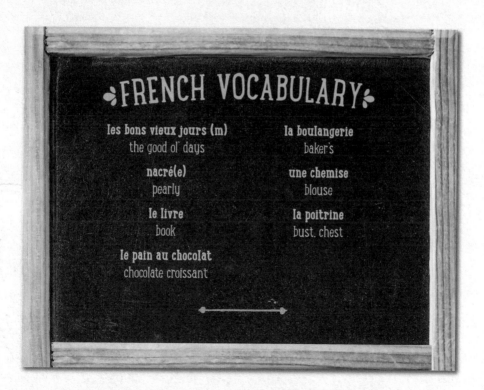

### ❧FRENCH VOCABULARY❧

**les bons vieux jours (m)**
the good ol' days

**nacré(e)**
pearly

**le livre**
book

**le pain au chocolat**
chocolate croissant

**la boulangerie**
baker's

**une chemise**
blouse

**la poitrine**
bust, chest

*Les tableaux*, or paintings, on the island of Groix—a popular vacation spot in Brittany.

# VADROUILLE

noun, feminine
(vah-drwee)

## A PURPOSELESS WALK, A WANDER

One hour before the sun slips behind the deep blue *Massif des Maures*, I ring my neighbor's doorbell.

"*On essaie un autre chemin aujourd'hui?*" I offer.

"*Pourquoi pas?*" replies my friend, Dominique, known to me affectionately as *La Voisine*. And off we march for our weekly chat-on-heels.

On the edge of our *voisinage*, our pace slows to accommodate the quiet scenery. We drift past a lone vineyard, its unkempt vines a contrast to the majestic castle in the darkening sky beyond.

We mosey down a dirt path flanked by sleeping fig trees, their dry *feuilles* having nodded off weeks ago.

We laugh as we amble past the free-range chickens scattering to and fro as if the French sky was falling toward their wrinkly feet.

We saunter toward the river to cross over a slender bridge no longer than an afternoon line at the post office. The river now at our backs, we hike the *chemin de terre* leading to the medieval village of Les Arcs-sur-Argens.

Above certain village doors we see dates etched into the stone *linteaux*: 1638... 1524....

"*Treizième, celui-là!*" La Voisine points out. I look up to admire another ancient doorway, grateful for the friend who has awakened

These half-curtains—seen everywhere in Provence—are known as *les brise-bise* (literally "break (the) wind").

this dreamer to another detail that might have gone unnoticed. How much more we take in when we walk with a pal! What might have been little more than a lazy stroll is now a study on all things historical.

We continue our *balade*, weaving through a maze of cobbled *ruelles*, walking where sewage once flowed as freely as village gossip, when families emptied their chamber pots into the narrow canal running down the center of the dirt roads.

We steal around another bend where the medieval village gives way to the colorful "modern" district. Gray stone walls meld into a slew of multicolored facades in pistachio green, custard yellow, and rum raisin red—village homes crammed together like so many colorful candies in a pack. Looking down, now, we see the cobblestone path is littered with bright red fruit—*les arbouses*.

Reaching down to pick up one of the bristly fruits, my own skin prickles with emotion for all that I have seen over the course of our improvised stroll.

"Take another path today," my mom always says. If you are reading, *Chère maman*, please know that I am.

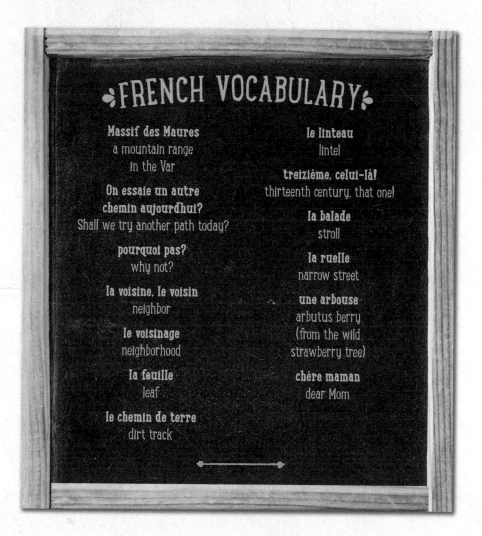

### ❧ FRENCH VOCABULARY ❧

**Massif des Maures**
a mountain range
in the Var

**On essaie un autre
chemin aujourd'hui?**
Shall we try another path today?

**pourquoi pas?**
why not?

**la voisine, le voisin**
neighbor

**le voisinage**
neighborhood

**la feuille**
leaf

**le chemin de terre**
dirt track

**le linteau**
lintel

**treizième, celui-là!**
thirteenth century, that one!

**la balade**
stroll

**la ruelle**
narrow street

**une arbouse**
arbutus berry
(from the wild
strawberry tree)

**chère maman**
dear Mom

*La Sardine D'Argile* (The Clay Sardine).
In the historic Panier neighborhood
of Marseilles, a painted *enseigne*, or sign,
hangs from a whimsical iron bar.

# SABOT

noun, masculine
(sah-bo)

## WOODEN SHOE, CLOG, SABOT

In the eighth *arrondissement* of Marseilles, at my mother-in-law's apartment complex, Jean-Marc and I climb several flights of stairs until we reach the last two doors in the building. One of the *portes* has a sign on it that reads *"peinture fraîche."* The wet paint warning causes us to automatically curl our shoulders inward and pull our suitcases close.

Jean-Marc slides *la clef* into the keyhole and pushes open the door to my *belle-mère's* one-bedroom apartment.

*"Vas-y,"* Go ahead, I say, trying to catch my breath after stepping off the French Stairmaster. We have just climbed four flights of stairs! How does my poor mother-in-law manage without an *ascenseur*?

My *belle-mère's* apartment, where we've come for a weekend getaway (Michèle-France is staying with the kids, at our place), carries me back to my first impressions of France, to the quirky things I'd forgotten (after having gotten rid of them, for comfort's sake), to the Frenchness that's worn off of things and places—the foreignness I wish would still pop out like so many doors on an Advent calendar, each with its own sweet cultural surprise.

All that stair climbing has caused me to work up a sweat. After leaving my overnight bag in the bedroom, I make my way to the *salle de bain* for a shower.

A *droguerie* and *quincaillerie* and *funeraire* shop —
or all-in-one hardware, junk, and funeral store. *Vive la France!*

I have to enter my *belle-mère's* tiny bathroom sideways, inching my way to the tub, known as *un sabot*, which in French means "slipper bath"—and for good reason: the bathtub is only slightly bigger than a *pantoufle!*

The tub has an unusual bi-level base: stand or sit. I choose to stand. Only, when I reach out to close the shower curtain, there isn't one. Oh yes, I'd forgotten about that: shower curtains are the exception in France!

A bit awkward in the curtainless *bain-douche,* I juggle the shampoo and the *savon*—all the while balancing a hand-held shower head so as not to flood the bathroom.

After the shower circus, I make coffee on one of those space-saving, three-in-one appliances where the lower drawer is a dishwasher, the middle section is an oven, and the burners are on top. I put water on to boil and go searching for a coffee mug; instead I find a stack of porcelain *bols* and am reminded that the French still drink their *café-au-lait* from a bowl, just as they still eat their cake with a spoon and not *une fourchette.*

I spend the rest of the weekend running into the Frenchness that I had left behind when we packed our bags and left Marseilles for the countryside ten years ago, for a home which has, over the years, gone from French to functional, from quirky to comfortable, from bi-level to... *banale.*

From the word *sabot* we get the verb *saboter*: "to bungle," or "to walk noisily." Come to think of it, it's no wonder I've become desensitized to the uniqueness that is France: I've been making too much noise and can no longer perceive it!

May this be a reminder to tiptoe past the Gallic culture that still whispers out from every French nook and cranny, to travel forward—light on my feet—so as not to "sabotage" this ever-unfolding French experience.

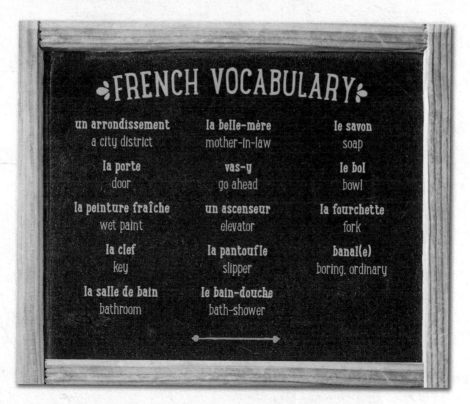

### ❖ FRENCH VOCABULARY ❖

| | | |
|---|---|---|
| **un arrondissement**<br>a city district | **la belle-mère**<br>mother-in-law | **le savon**<br>soap |
| **la porte**<br>door | **vas-y**<br>go ahead | **le bol**<br>bowl |
| **la peinture fraîche**<br>wet paint | **un ascenseur**<br>elevator | **la fourchette**<br>fork |
| **la clef**<br>key | **la pantoufle**<br>slipper | **banal(e)**<br>boring, ordinary |
| **la salle de bain**<br>bathroom | **le bain-douche**<br>bath-shower | |

*Les oursins*, or sea urchins, and a glass of rosé wine from Domaine Rouge-Bleu, where Jean-Marc created *un domaine viticole*, or wine growing estate in 2007.

# OURSIN

noun. masculine
(or-sehn)

## SEA URCHIN

At a sandy Mediterranean *crique* near the town of Les Issambres—separated from St. Raphaël by a deep blue gulf—we closed our weekend on a rich, sea-salty note. If you factored out the cloudless sky, you'd see how the reddish blur of the Esterel mountains capped the busy French city *en face* like an Arizona sunset.

During the half-hour drive from our village to *la plage*, I quizzed Jean-Marc on his favorite delicacy.

"Do you know the other French term for *oursin*?" I said.

To my surprise, he only knew the one word. "*Une châtaigne de mer!*" I answered, pleased to know something French that he didn't. When Jean-Marc found the term 'sea chestnut' endearing, I offered him the English equivalent: "sea hedgehog."

As my masked Frenchman headed out to sea to hunt the underwater hedgehogs, I wished him "*Bonne oursinade!*"

"That will come later," he reminded me with a smile.

True, an *oursinade* is the "feasting on sea urchins" and not the hunting of sea urchins.

"*Alors, BONNE PÊCHE!*" Happy fishing! I called out.

Apart from the mask, Jean-Marc wore thick rubber sandals and carried his formidable mop-spear (half mop stick, half fork—a do-it-yourself tool he'd rigged together on a previous expedition). I notice he'd swiped my laundry basket, too, and was dragging that out to sea as well....

Eventually, Max and Jackie swam out to the tiny rock island and helped their father collect the "sea chestnuts." Jean-Marc returned first, barefoot, followed by the kids who'd tucked a half-dozen *oursins* into their father's size 12 plastic shoes before floating their catch back to shore.

The four of us sat on our beach towels, admiring the spiny creatures in the laundry basket. Beneath the setting sun the urchins showed their brilliant colors in copper, violet, and khaki.

Jean-Marc used shearing scissors (another steal from our bathroom, along with the *panier à linge*) to open the prickly spears, revealing a star pattern inside. The sea urchin eggs were nestled there, *dans l'étoile*.

"*Bon appétit!*" one passerby called out.

We didn't have spoons and were obliged to lick the strips of orange roe from the shell, taking care not to get stabbed by an *épine* in the process.

I watched my husband savor the delicate orange "fruits of the sea," washing the roe down with a splash of rosé wine.

"*Rien de plus simple,*" he said. "*Rien de meilleur.*"

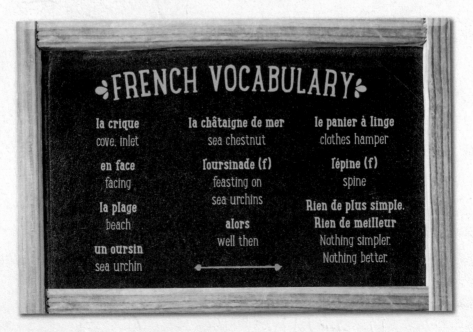

**⁂FRENCH VOCABULARY⁂**

| | | |
|---|---|---|
| **la crique**<br>cove, inlet | **la châtaigne de mer**<br>sea chestnut | **le panier à linge**<br>clothes hamper |
| **en face**<br>facing | **l'oursinade (f)**<br>feasting on<br>sea urchins | **l'épine (f)**<br>spine |
| **la plage**<br>beach | | **Rien de plus simple.**<br>**Rien de meilleur**<br>Nothing simpler. |
| **un oursin**<br>sea urchin | **alors**<br>well then | Nothing better. |

Soccer mania! In the pottery-making town of Salernes,
an old cheese shop boasts a new sporty sign:
*"Allez OM!"* (Go Olympique de Marseilles!)

*Une écurie*, or horse stable, near the village of Le Muy. The van, or *le fourgon*, is an old Citroën.

# COLLECTE DE FONDS

noun, feminine
(koh-lekt-deuh-fohn)

## FUNDRAISING

‖sped up to the *trottoir* before easing my car's right front tire onto the curb. Next, I inched the vehicle forward until the second tire climbed up, level with the first. *Voilà*, curbside parking *à la française*.

As I waited in the warm *bagnole* for my children's school to let out, my eyes traveled up to the window in the *bâtiment* across the street. Each day I park my car as mentioned and each day I look for the grandma in the window. There, behind the chipped flowerpots with their thirsty, petal-thinning *marguerites*, beyond the dull window and the parted lace curtains, I see her soft outline. That's when I lower the volume on my radio, not wanting to disturb *la mémé* in the window.

This afternoon two men, dressed identically in navy blue uniforms and black steel-toed boots, approached *la porte* just below Mémé's window and rang the *sonnette*. I looked up, noting Mémé had disappeared from behind the curtain. *She must be on her way down the stairs to open the door*, I thought. Anticipation grew as I realized I was about to see the full version of Mémé and not just a puff of gray hair and a dark profile.

The men continued to ring when, upon closer look, I realized they might be paramedics. "Mémé!" I rolled down my window and shouted, *"Elle est là! Je l'ai vue! Allez-y—foncez!"* She's there! I saw her! Go ahead—*charge on in*!

*"Merci, madame,"* they replied, casually. That's when I saw the calendars under one of the *pompier's* arms. And then it clicked. Mémé hadn't fallen ill. Mémé was hiding from the firemen, trying to avoid the annual *collecte de fonds*, or 10 euros for the Firefighter Fundraising Calendar. And she might have gone unnoticed had not a clueless *bonne Samaritaine* gone and blown her cover.

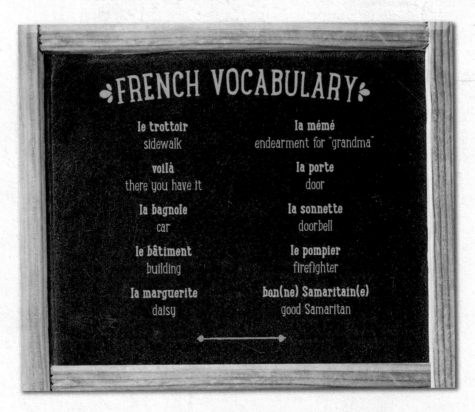

**❖FRENCH VOCABULARY❖**

**le trottoir**
sidewalk

**la mémé**
endearment for "grandma"

**voilà**
there you have it

**la porte**
door

**la bagnole**
car

**la sonnette**
doorbell

**le bâtiment**
building

**le pompier**
firefighter

**la marguerite**
daisy

**bon(ne) Samaritain(e)**
good Samaritan

This horseshoe, in Figanières, is sure
to bring good luck. But what will
the lovely pinecones attract?

*Chez le ferronnier.* At the ironworker's shop there is a whimsical, framed portfolio of the artist's products.

# PINCEAU

noun, masculine
(pehn-so)

## PAINTBRUSH

Breezing past our living room, Jean-Marc is wearing a long African robe and a five o'clock shadow. In his left hand he is holding a small can of touch-up paint and in his right, a wet paintbrush.

I have grown to accept my husband's taste in lounge wear and the fact that he sees no reason to change into work clothes for his latest DIY project.

For a nostalgic moment I remember back to when he bought that robe, or *boubou*. It was in '92, during one of his *missions d'audit* in Africa. Though he did not like his short stint as an accountant, he loved Djibouti. When he wasn't stuck in an office verifying spreadsheets at a local petroleum company, Jean-Marc enjoyed fishing with the locals in a deep, blue bay along the sea.

"*Ça va*, Mr. Touch-up?" I tease, following my husband through the house. I can't help but want to put in my two cents' worth. "You missed a spot! *T'as oublié celle-là!*"

The man in the robe responds by playfully poking me in the nose with the wet end of the *pinceau*. When I complain, he counters: "*C'est lavable à l'eau.*"

Moving quickly through our little house, Jean-Marc brushes paint over child-size fingerprints and across chipped baseboards in a quest to cover up grease marks, scuffs, and smudges.

"Grab a paintbrush!" he calls, when passing by the kids' rooms. "*Allez, on y va!*"

Because Mr. Touch-up forgets to mention where he's been, the kids and I are never sure just which surfaces are wet and when to watch out. It is the cream-colored streak across the seat of my pants (where I've backed into a wet wall) or beneath Max's palm or on Jackie's fingertip that reminds us that the touch-up artist has struck again. *Touché!*

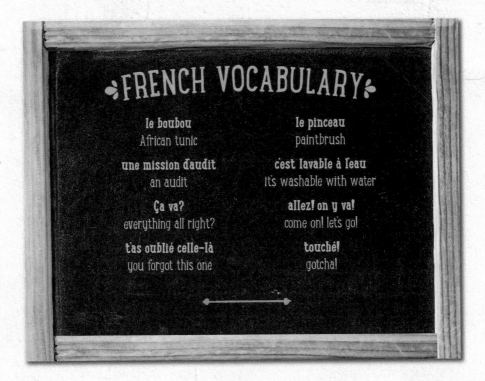

**❀ FRENCH VOCABULARY ❀**

| | |
|---|---|
| **le boubou** | **le pinceau** |
| African tunic | paintbrush |
| **une mission d'audit** | **c'est lavable à l'eau** |
| an audit | it's washable with water |
| **Ça va?** | **allez! on y va!** |
| everything all right? | come on! let's go! |
| **t'as oublié celle-là** | **touché!** |
| you forgot this one | gotcha! |

This sun-kissed beauty lives in the
town of La Motte. just across the
street from the beekeeper's.

In fond memory of
George Whitman
12 December 1913 - 14 December 2011

"...the business of books is the business of life."

37 Rue de la Bûcherie, 75005 Paris, France—
home of Shakespeare and Company bookstore.
Among the lovable and inspiring characters I have
had the chance to meet, was a famously hospitable—
and often irascible—bookshop owner who
encouraged writers and readers and vagabonds.
"*Adieu*, George Whitman."

# PISSENLIT

noun, masculine
(pee-sahn-lee)

## DANDELION

The French have a colorful expression for "dead and buried": *manger les pissenlits par les racines* ("to eat dandelions by the roots"). Will I one day be buried here in this French necropolis? The question haunts me each time I set foot in a *cimetière*. Though France feels more like home than Phoenix, I couldn't be more misplaced than in this French graveyard!

The Mistral wind is sweeping through the *cimetière* here in Les Arcs-sur-Argens. Strolling alone on an afternoon walk, I am amazed to see parts of the medieval burial site literally lift off! When you live in a 12th-century village, I guess you can expect a crumbling graveyard. *What crumbles turns to dust...* I think, eerily, and begin to wonder whether it is this dust that is making me cough as I make my way through the maze of carved stone and iron.

I look around the medieval cemetery at the tombstones, the freestanding mausoleums, the barren plots topped with gravel—plots so old that the names have disappeared from the headstones, or the stones have disappeared altogether after cracking, crumbling and finally being carried off by the wind. On top of many of the graves, only a lopsided cross remains. In one corner of the graveyard there is a pile of broken stone, bits and pieces of statues that have fallen from certain plots, crashed to the ground, only to be swept together in one big heap. I wonder what the groundskeeper is planning on doing with these "ornaments." I think about how such relics are an antiquarian's gold mine (in fact, *wouldn't that broken cherub's wing look great in my bedroom?*). I kick myself for letting such an odd thought cross through my mind.

Redirecting my imagination, it occurs to me that I'll truly be anchored to France the day I lie down *pour de bon*. Might as well get to know my future neighbors.... I look at the names on the tombstones: Famille Charrier, Famille Audibert, Famille Bressin.... I am an Ingham by birth—*Famille Ingham*. I think about the cemetery in Seattle where the Inghams are buried. Somehow it doesn't seem like a place to spend eternity on earth either.

Well, what about Phoenix? I try to remember whether I have ever seen a cemetery in The Valley of the Sun. Cemeteries in the desert are so... *hidden*, not like in France—where the subterranean *dortoirs* exist at the top of every picturesque village.

No, I don't want to be stuck out in the desert, with nothing but a scrawny desert rat scrambling by, or a few lazy tumbleweeds bumping into my headstone before tumbling on to Tucson.

Maybe I'll be buried in Fuveau, near Aix-en-Provence? That is where the Espinasse family rests. I now realize I have never met any of the family buried there. No, this is no final home for the future *moi* either.

Perhaps it is the "forever" aspect that bothers me? As it is, I can leave France whenever I choose to, return to the desert whenever I wish. But once I hit *subterranean France* my vagabond days will be over!

Standing alone, I look around at the cramped grave site, and realize—not without *soulagement*—that there is no room within this walled community for me. And, just as it always is when I begin to fret about the outcome of things, Madame Here and Monsieur Now appear, in time to offer a needed reminder. I take the hint and reach down to pluck up a stray dandelion....

"*Souffle!*" Madame Here and Monsieur Now command. "Blow!"

I take a deep breath and let go....

The dandelion trembles as I once have. Watching the seeds fly off, so many tiny encapsulated "what ifs" now scatter toward the sun and gently disappear.

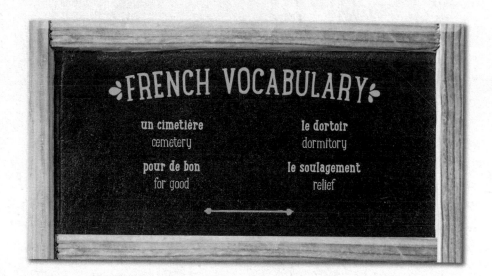

❖FRENCH VOCABULARY❖

| un cimetière | le dortoir |
|---|---|
| cemetery | dormitory |
| pour de bon | le soulagement |
| for good | relief |

*Au revoir.* Goodbye for now. These hats. or *chapeaux.* remind me of some of the characters we've met in the previous pages. Which hat would my *belle-mère* wear. while delivering her chocolate cake? What about Jean-Marc. for his sea urchin expeditions?
For me... is there a newsboy cap to wear while writing? And don't forget Françoise. who closed her art store. I see her in the purple one. right! (The straw one just below has my mom's name on it!) Is there a butterfly hat for Bobby. who is sitting beneath the cherry tree? Which other *personnages.* or characters do you recall? May they whisper to you. *en français.* when you dream at night.

# ENTRETIEN

noun, masculine
(ontr-tee-en)

## INTERVIEW

Janet Skeslien Charles, author of the novel *Moonlight in Odessa*, chatted with me about the writing process. Here is an excerpt from our conversation.

## WHAT BROUGHT YOU TO FRANCE?

An exchange program during my third year at Arizona State University. I had fallen in love with all things French around the age of 12. As a sophomore in high school, I took my first French class but lost heart after almost failing it. Happily, there are second chances in life! Mine came when a certain teacher encouraged me to look past my shortcomings in the language—and dive into the culture! (I'll never forget you, Madame Wollam!)

## WHAT KEEPS YOU IN FRANCE?

The brightly painted window shutters with pots of geraniums on the sill, the rickety old bicycles with saggy saddlebags on the side, my mother-in-law's tapenade and a love of the language—especially *parapluie*, *chouchou*, and *c'est la vie*.

## WHY DID YOU START YOUR BLOG?

I was looking for a place in cyberspace to "pin up" my stories. Only, having posted them, no one came over to read—until I lured them in with the promise of a "word a day." Because I love to infuse stories with French, a French word-a-day was the perfect carrot!

## WHAT ADVICE WOULD YOU GIVE TO SOMEONE WHO IS THINKING OF STARTING A BLOG?

"Just do it!" as Nike says. So many people feel they need to wait until they have gathered together some stories. Don't wait! Start now, today! Next, never take the reader for granted. They are investing time into reading your post, so make it informational, visually satisfying, and entertaining.

## WHAT IS THE BEST ADVICE YOU HAVE EVER RECEIVED?

To risk. *Take risks in your writing!*

## CAN YOU TELL US ABOUT YOUR PATH TO PUBLICATION?

I began blogging in 2002, sending out a daily word and a corresponding story. Within two months I had collected enough vignettes to make a book, which I self-published. I called this publishing venture "Four Frogs Press" (my husband, two children, and I being the "frogs"). I then put up a Paypal button on my site encouraging readers to pre-order the book—which I was still busy putting together! This way I earned money for the first print run— all of 25 books! By the second book ("Words in a French Life, Volume II"), the print run went to 250. And by the third installation ("Volume III"…) I was ordering 500 books and creating book packages, encouraging readers to *"Save when you buy all three!"*

One day I received an email from an editor at Simon and Schuster. They were interested in working together! I learned that a journalist in Beijing had sent my blog address to an editor in NYC. The journalist was Ann Mah (author of *Mastering the Art of French Eating*) and the editor was Amanda Patten. It was a dream come true to work with a major publishing house, which printed a hardbound cdition of my book *Words in a French Life: Lessons in Love and Language in the South of France.*

## HOW DOES LIVING IN A FOREIGN COUNTRY AFFECT YOUR WRITING?

Living in France gives me an immediate topic, one that I would not have otherwise found as a beginning writer. (There is always that question: "What to write about?" It stalls writers to no end!) Here, in Provence, there is something to write about the minute you step out the door: the Vélosolex moped that just whizzed by, as it might have in post-war France; and the retiring farmer who is ringing the bell at our front gate, wondering if we want to buy his grapes. These same subjects exist worldwide, but it sometimes takes living in a foreign land to find one's surroundings exotic. The trick is to see the ordinary through a traveler's lens—to be in exile in one's own country.

## WHAT DOES IT ADD TO YOUR WRITING?

Vocabulary! The best thing about writing from a foreign country is the chance to infuse one's story with the language of the land. I love to drop French words into the stories, in context—making it easy to figure out the meaning without straining for a dictionary.

## WHAT IS YOUR FAVORITE PLACE TO WRITE?

In my office. It's the quietest place in the house—except for the cicadas screeching outside the window or my husband who shouts when his favorite soccer team (L'OM) makes a goal. And there's an issue with bees and nesting. I have learned to type while the bees do their *aller-retours* right beneath my nose, buzzing back and forth from the window to the bookshelf, where they are "building something." I figure we are both building something: stories, beehives, *a life that thrives.*

That's not a real mailbox but a *trompe-l'oeil*.
And this is Robert Farjon. Let's meet him, finally....

Cher Monsieur Farjon,
  Merci pour votre photo.
Ce dernier chapitre est pour
vous, traduit en français
pour que vous le compreniez.
Bonne lecture.

    Amicalement,
    Kristi

# A NOTE ABOUT THE COVER OF THIS BOOK

(The following letter was published in my online journal, just before this book's publication)

*Chers Amis et Amies,*

Thank you for responding to my note about the recent setback in my book project, "First French *Essais*." I heeded your words, took a breather and let my book angels, Erin and Tamara, work their magic. With the wave of a wand Erin ordered me to shoo!, or *allez zou!*, while she and Tami got to work. "Go turn on some Bob Marley..." Erin ordered, via email, adding with a smiley face, "Don't worry about a thing, 'Cause every little thing gonna be all right..." : )

Now that the book angels had my back once again, I was free to consider a needed addition to the manuscript: attribution!

*Heavens!* The book might have gone to print and you wouldn't even know who the model was on the cover! This wasn't the only *pépin*, or glitch to my book release. I still needed to ask my accidental model for permission to use his photo. My sneaky picture-cropping gesture, designed to protect his privacy, had its glaring weaknesses: *that plant* for one, a dead giveaway! Though some of you—during the book cover vote—mistook it for a stack of letters (interesting how the painted mailbox, located center

# UN MOT SUR LA COUVERTURE DU LIVRE

(La lettre suivante a été publiée dans mon journal en ligne.
juste avant la publication de ce livre)

Chers Amis et Amies,

Merci d'avoir répondu à ma note sur le récent délai dans mon projet de livre, « Premiers Essais Français ». J'ai tenu compte de vos mots, pris une pause et laissé mes «Anges de livres», Erin et Tamara, utiliser leur pouvoir magique. D'un coup de baguette, Erin m'a chassé *ouste !*, ou allez, zou!, tandis qu'elle et Tami se mettaient au travail. « Va jouer du Bob Marley », Erin m'a gentiment ordonné par courriel, ajoutant un smiley : «Don't worry about a thing, 'Cause every little thing gonna be all right» :-)

Maintenant que les «Anges de livres» prenaient la responsabilité de mon livre, j'étais libre d'envisager un supplément nécessaire pour le manuscrit : reconnaissance !

Mon Dieu ! Le livre aurait pu partir à l'impression et vous n'auriez même pas su qui était le modèle sur la couverture ! Ce n'était pas le seul pépin, ou souci à résoudre avant la sortie de mon livre. J'avais encore besoin de demander la permission à mon modèle « de hasard » d'utiliser sa photo. Mon geste photographique un peu sournois, conçu pour protéger sa vie privée, avait des faiblesses flagrantes : en premier, cette plante était une vraie révélation ! Bien que certains d'entre vous — lors du vote de la couverture du livre — ont confondu la plante avec une pile de lettres (intéressant de voir comment la boîte aux lettres peinte, située au centre de la

picture, played tricks on your minds!), the plant was an obvious clue-in as to who is the well-known village figure on the cover.

To understand why, I'll need to take you back to the summer my family moved to Sainte Cécile-les-Vignes. Back then, my husband was embarking on his wine adventure, having found 9 hectares of vines to tend. As Jean-Marc set about discovering the *terroir*, I stepped out to discover our new village.

## THE PLANT MAN

It was at the Saturday farmers market that I first laid eyes on Monsieur Farjon. I was mesmerized. There he was, two, three fruit stands away from me—standing at the head of the outdoor produce aisle chatting with a farmer.

Looking at this photo today I smile, shaking my head seeing that *even then* he was handing out plants to the locals, expounding on (just look at his passionate gestures!) the organic treasures that could be found along the gutter or in the weedy field relegated to the electric company or beside the busy roadway leading into Sainte Cécile. It seemed that some of the villagers regarded him as an eccentric.

This made the man all the more endearing in my eyes. Almost as attractive as that bike! If there are two things in this world I love it is antique bicycles and strong French characters. But a new realm was soon to open up to me and, with it, a third thing in this world to love: *plants!*

photo, vous a joué des tours !), la plante était un indice évident pour identifier, sur la couverture, ce personnage bien connu du village.

Pour comprendre pourquoi, je devrais vous ramener à l'été 2007, quand ma famille a déménagé à Sainte Cécile-les-Vignes. À l'époque, mon mari se lançait dans son aventure du vin, ayant trouvé 9 hectares de vignes à cultiver. Pendant que Jean-Marc se lançait à la découverte du terroir, je suis partie à la découverte de notre nouveau village.

## L'HOMME DES PLANTES

C'était au marché des fermiers du samedi que j'ai posé pour la première fois les yeux sur Monsieur Farjon. J'étais fascinée. Il était là, à deux ou trois étals de fruits de moi — au bout de l'allée des fruits et légumes en train de bavarder avec un agriculteur.

En regardant cette photo aujourd'hui, je souris en secouant la tête de voir que, même alors qu'il distribuait des plantes à la population locale, il donnait un exposé (regardez ses gestes passionnés !) sur les trésors biologiques qui pouvaient être trouvés le long des rigoles ou dans le domaine des mauvaises herbes abandonné à l'Électricité de France ou encore à côté de la route menant à Sainte Cécile. Il me semblait que certains des villageois le considérait comme quelqu'un d'original.

Cela rendait cet homme d'autant plus attachant à mes yeux. Presque aussi intéressant que son vélo ! Il y a deux choses que j'aime dans ce monde : les vélos anciens et les caractères français forts. Mais un nouveau royaume allait bientôt s'ouvrir à moi et, avec lui, une troisième chose à aimer ici-bas : *les plantes!*

I did not approach Monsieur Farjon there at the market that day. I quickly snapped his photo and hurried off—lest he chase me down with that splendid vehicle and confiscate my camera!

Meantime—without ever having known whose photo it was I had taken—a spell had come over me. *I began to notice leafy things.* Specifically I developed an obsession for a certain pink (and sometimes white) wildflower growing in the most unexpected places: jutting vertically out of rock walls and coming up through cracks in the pavement. Could it be a weed? What a gorgeous *mauvaise herbe* at that! It would be perfect in my garden (currently a pile of rocks). If that plant could push through concrete it could populate my barren yard!

One day while driving home from Bollène, I saw the weed-flower growing beside a telephone pole. At the same moment, I saw a farmer walking along the road. *Chances are that guy would have information about the plant!* I thought, running my car off the road and hurrying up to the stranger.

Je n'ai pas abordé M. Farjon au marché ce jour-là. J'ai rapidement pris sa photo et je me suis dépêchée de filer — de peur qu'il ne me pourchasse avec son splendide véhicule et confisque mon appareil photo !

Entre-temps — sans jamais savoir de qui j'avais pris la photo — un sortilège m'avait été jeté. J'ai commencé à remarquer « les choses feuillues ». Plus précisément, j'ai développé une obsession pour une certaine fleur sauvage rose (et parfois blanche) poussant dans les endroits les plus inattendus : saillant verticalement des murs en pierre et jaillissant à travers les fissures de la chaussée. Serait-ce une mauvaise herbe ? Quelle magnifique mauvaise herbe ! Elle serait parfaite dans mon jardin (à ce moment-là un tas de pierres). Si cette plante pouvait pousser à travers le béton elle pourrait peupler surement ma cour stérile !

Un jour, alors que je revenais chez moi en voiture de Bollène, j'ai revu la mauvaise-herbe-fleur poussant à côté d'un poteau téléphonique. Au même moment, je remarquais un paysan marchant le long de la route. *C'est possible que ce gars ait des informations sur cette plante !,* pensais-je tout en garant ma voiture au bord de la route et en me dépêchant pour rattraper cet étranger.

# SERENDIPITOUS MEETING

"That guy" turned out to be Robert Farjon. Not only had I stumbled onto the man I'd seen at the market, but I was about to learn, over the course of the next year, the extent of one man's knowledge of the Provençal plant kingdom—beginning with *le lilas d'Espagne*.

"Lily of Spain. That's just its common name," Monsieur Farjon explained. "It is officially known as 'valerian'."

Our brief encounter led to a surprise visit, when Mr Farjon rode his bike to our vineyard, a good dozen or two farm fields from the village. His bike's saddlebags were bursting with my next lesson: euphorbia, *prêle*, and physalis, or "love in a cage." Monsieur Farjon passed me a leafy bundle, as though handing over a delicate newborn, and so transmitted his instinct to protect and to revere *les plantes*.

Those weekly (Tuesday) lessons—or *"Mardis avec Monsieur Farjon"*—lasted three seasons: spring, summer, fall. It was cold and windy the next-to-last-time Monsieur Farjon rode his bike from Sainte Cécile all the way out to our farm. But we still saw each other, often crossing paths in the village. He always had a leafy example tucked in his pocket or hat band or in those saddlebags. He was ever prepared to share about plants.

# HEUREUX HASARD DE RENCONTRE

« Ce gars » s'est avéré être Robert Farjon. Non seulement j'étais tombée sur l'homme que j'avais vu au marché, mais j'étais sur le point d'apprendre, au cours de la prochaine année, l'ampleur des connaissances de cet homme sur le sujet du règne végétal Provençal — en commençant par *le lilas d'Espagne*.

« Lilas d'Espagne. C'est son nom commun », m'a expliqué M. Farjon. « Il est officiellement connu comme *valériane*. »

Notre brève rencontre a mené à une visite surprise, lorsque M. Farjon est monté en vélo vers notre vignoble, à une bonne douzaine ou deux de champs de fermes du village. Les sacoches gonflées de son vélo débordaient des sujets de ma prochaine leçon : euphorbe, prêle, et physalis ou « L'amour en cage ». Monsieur Farjon me donnait un bouquet de verdure, comme s'il me remettait un nouveau-né fragile, et ainsi me transmettait son instinct de protection et de vénération *des plantes*.

Ces leçons hebdomadaires du mardi, ou « Mes Mardis avec Monsieur Farjon », ont duré trois saisons : printemps, été, automne. Il faisait froid et venteux l'avant-dernière fois où M. Farjon est monté en vélo depuis Sainte Cécile et a pris le long chemin jusqu'à notre ferme. Mais nous nous sommes revus encore, nous croisant souvent dans les rues du village. Il avait toujours un échantillon verdoyant niché dans sa poche ou dans la bande de son chapeau ou bien dans ses sacoches. Il était toujours enchanté de partager son savoir des plantes.

During *la fête du livre* Monsieur Farjon visited me at my book stand in Sainte Cécile. His old bike held two saddlebags full of just-picked plants! When book sales were sluggish we spent the time studying acanthus, milkweed, and lunaria—to the amusement of the bookworms who filed by our leafy stand.

No matter how rushed I always lent my ear, listening closely as he stuttered the name of the species in question shar-shar-*shar-don mah-ree* (chardon marie or "milk thistle"). His slight *bégaiement* only made him more endearing, and it was an exercise in French to coax those botanical words out of his mouth.

As I turn this book over and look at the photo on the back, I'm reminded of one of our last encounters. I can't quite identify the flower he is holding (*les immortelles*? How symbolic!), for that day I was more focused on the beholder. Just how many more chance meetings would there be?

Soon after, we decided to move and my last visit with Monsieur Farjon mirrored the first. There he was on the side of the road, near a patch of wild *dents de lion*. I ran my car off the road and hurried across the street, feeling as scattered as a dandelion seed.

"Monsieur Farjon. I'm moving. It's been such a pleasure to know you!" At loss for a meaningful way to say goodbye, I reached down and gently plucked what some would regard as a pesky weed.

Durant la fête du livre de Sainte Cécile, M. Farjon rendu visite à mon stand de livres. Son vieux vélo portait deux sacoches pleines de plantes fraîchement cueillies ! Lorsque les ventes de livres étaient plus calmes nous passions le temps à étudier : l'acanthe, l'asclépiade et la lunaire — à l'amusement des rats de bibliothèque qui défilaient devant notre stand feuillu.

Peu importe à quel point j'étais pressée, j'ai toujours prêté l'oreille, écoutant attentivement, alors qu'il bégayait le nom de l'espèce en question char-char-char-don ma-rie (Chardon-Marie). Son léger bégaiement me le rendait encore plus attachant, et c'était tout un exercice en français pour lui soutirer ces mots botaniques de la bouche.

Quand je retourne ce livre et que je regarde la photo au dos, je me souviens d'une de nos dernières rencontres. Je ne peux pas tout à fait identifier la fleur qu'il tient (les immortelles ? Comme c'est symbolique !), car ce jour-là j'étais plus concentrée sur celui qui tenait la fleur. Combien d'autres rencontres de hasard y aurait-il encore ?

Peu après, nous avons décidé de déménager, ma dernière rencontre avec M. Farjon était comme le miroir de la première. Il était là, sur le côté de la route, près d'un parterre de dents-de-lion. J'ai garé ma voiture sur le bord de la route et me suis précipitée dans la rue, me sentant aussi éparpillée qu'une graine de pissenlit.

« M. Farjon, je vais déménager ! Ça m'a fait vraiment plaisir de vous connaitre ! » Comme je n'arrivais pas à trouver la bonne manière de lui dire au revoir, je me suis baissée et cueillis délicatement ce que certains considèrent comme une mauvaise herbe gênante.

Handing Monsieur the vibrant yellow flower that is strong enough to break free through concrete, I listened as The Plant Man broke my heart.

"*Adieu,*" Monsieur Farjon said with simplicity and with warmth.

*See you in heaven?* So that was it? Did he not wish to see me again—or was he only being a realist? (Pedaling his bike from the village to our farm was one thing, but riding all the way to Mediterranean Sea.... No, not a possibility!)

After we moved to our new village, near Bandol, Jean-Marc began another vineyard and I focused on my writing, collecting together stories from our time in Les Arcs-sur-Argens (before we moved to Sainte Cécile). When it came time to design a book cover, I stumbled once again across Monsieur Farjon—this time in my photo archives.

*No, I couldn't use his picture...* or if I did I'd have to ask. *That meant I would have to contact him*—Mr. See You in Heaven! But what if he was already in heaven?

No, I didn't want to find out. Then one morning last week I got up the courage to call his niece at her vineyard. This time *I* was the one stuttering.

"Je... je... *je voudrais utiliser l'image de ton oncle....*"

Mireille said she would pass along the message and get back with me. A few days after that I received this letter by email:

Remettant à Monsieur la fleur jaune vibrante, cette fleur capable de retrouver sa liberté à travers le béton, j'écoutais alors que L'homme des Plantes me brisait le coeur.

« Adieu », me disait M. Farjon avec simplicité et chaleur.

*Rendez-vous au paradis ?*
C'était donc ça ? Ne voulait-il plus me voir — ou était-il seulement réaliste ? Il est vrai que rouler en vélo du village à la ferme était une chose, mais pédaler tout le chemin jusqu'à la mer Méditerranée .... Non, ce n'est pas possible !

Après avoir déménagé dans notre nouveau village près de Bandol, Jean-Marc a commencé à cultiver un autre vignoble pendant que je me concentrais sur mon écriture, collectionnant les histoires de notre période à Les Arcs-sur-Argens (avant que nous déménagions à Sainte Cécile).

Quand est venu le temps de concevoir une couverture de livre, je suis tombée une fois de plus sur M. Farjon — cette fois en fouillant mes archives de photos.

Non, je ne pouvais pas utiliser son image ... ou si je le faisais, je devais lui demander sa permission. Cela voulait dire que je devais contacter « M. Rendez-vous au ciel » ! Mais que faire s'il était déjà au ciel ?

Non, je ne voulais pas découvrir ça. Puis, un matin de la semaine dernière, j'ai eu le courage d'appeler sa nièce à son vignoble. Cette fois-ci, c'était moi qui bégayais.

« Je ... je ... je voudrais utiliser l'image de ton oncle ... »

Mireille me dit qu'elle allait lui transmettre le message et me rappeler. Quelques jours après, j'ai reçu cette lettre par courriel :

*Hello, Kristi,*

*Just saw Robert this morning and I showed him your project. He is entirely OK with your printing his photo. He holds a wonderful memory of your passage in Sainte Cécile. He told me he has written a hundred or so botanical papers and dropped them off at the cultural center in Sainte Cécile.*

*See you soon,*

*Mireille*

I, too, hold a wonderful memory of Monsieur Farjon and I look forward to sharing more with you in the follow up to this book (a story about our *passage* in Sainte Cécile-les-Vignes…).

And so, as Mireille says, *à bientôt!*

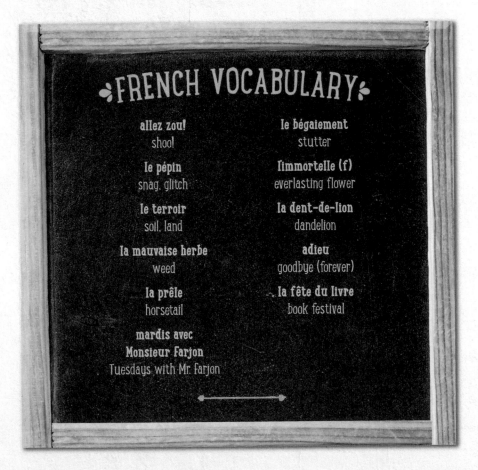

❖FRENCH VOCABULARY❖

**allez zou!**
shoo!

**le pépin**
snag, glitch

**le terroir**
soil, land

**la mauvaise herbe**
weed

**la prêle**
horsetail

**mardis avec
Monsieur Farjon**
Tuesdays with Mr. Farjon

**le bégaiement**
stutter

**l'immortelle (f)**
everlasting flower

**la dent-de-lion**
dandelion

**adieu**
goodbye (forever)

**la fête du livre**
book festival

*Bonjour, Kristi,*

*J'ai vu Robert ce matin et je lui ai montré ton projet. Il est tout à fait d'accord pour que tu imprimes sa photo. Il garde un très bon souvenir de ton passage à Ste Cécile. Il m'a dit qu'il avait créé une centaine de fiches botaniques et qu'il les avait déposées à l'Espace Culturel de Ste Cécile.*

*A très bientôt,*

*Mireille*

Moi aussi, je garde un merveilleux souvenir de Monsieur Farjon et je suis impatiente de partager encore plus de nouvelles expériences avec vous dans le livre suivant (l'histoire de notre passage à Sainte Cécile -les-Vignes ...)

Et alors, comme le dit Mireille, *à bientôt !*

*Un troupeau de moutons,* or a flock of sheep, in Les Arcs-sur-Argens.

Like little *drapeaux prières*, or prayer flags, these colorful squares make up a creative shop sign in Brignoles.

# LES MOTS CACHÉS

Many thanks to Kim Steele at www.puzzles-to-print.com for creating this word search to help recall and memorize French vocabulary! To complete the puzzle, review the chapter titles in this book and search for them here:

```
S  D  N  O  F  E  D  E  T  C  E  L  L  O  C  T  R
P  P  I  S  S  E  N  L  I  T  C  O  H  C  K  M  A
Y  E  C  I  M  J  M  T  R  A  P  E  R  I  A  F  F
I  L  Z  A  T  N  A  S  S  I  V  A  R  F  H  E  R
M  L  E  Q  F  X  E  M  P  L  E  T  T  E  S  B  A
X  I  R  E  N  A  L  P  I  K  R  E  X  P  R  E  N
E  U  U  J  P  A  R  I  E  R  E  A  Z  I  H  P  G
R  O  T  E  P  M  N  D  K  G  S  X  L  C  X  A  I
V  R  I  E  N  E  T  I  R  V  T  L  E  L  T  Q  N
I  D  R  C  N  T  C  N  S  S  E  P  X  U  A  U  E
U  A  R  A  S  G  R  P  A  R  S  W  P  N  E  E  B
S  V  U  W  M  Z  I  E  D  R  U  O  G  E  S  G  B
R  J  O  V  N  D  Y  D  T  A  R  O  A  T  S  G  O
U  V  P  W  O  H  C  W  N  I  A  A  O  T  A  L  U
O  R  U  A  E  C  N  I  P  I  E  I  M  E  B  V  D
P  L  A  I  S  S  E  L  L  E  L  N  U  S  O  I  E
F  S  P  U  D  N  E  T  N  E  L  A  M  F  T  L  R
```

| | | | |
|---|---|---|---|
| Aisselle | Entretien | Marrant | Planer |
| Bouder | Faire-Part | Oursin | Pourriture |
| Briller | Frangine | Pâques | Poursuivre |
| Cafard | Gourde | Parier | Ravissant |
| Choc | Indigne | Pêche | Restes |
| Collecte de Fonds | Lunettes | Pinceau | Sabot |
| Emplette | Malentendu | Pissenlit | Toile |
| | | | Vadrouille |

Adding to France's charm and attraction
are the classic fishing boats, or *pointus*.
This wooden boat lives in the *presqu'île*,
or peninsula, of Giens.

# LES MOTS CACHÉS
## SOLUTION

```
S D N O F E D E T C E L L O C T R A
P P I S S E N L I T C O H C K M R A
Y E C I M J M T R A P E R I A F E F
I Z A T N A S S I V A R F H E R R
M E Q F X E M P L E T T E S R B A
X R E N A L P I K R E X P R E N
E U J P A R I E R E A Z I H P G
R T E P M N D K G S X L C X A I
V I E N E T I R V T L E T P N
I R C N T C N S E P X N A E
U U R S G R P A R S W P N B
S O A W M Z I E D R U O G E B
R P V M N D Y D T A R O A T O
U O W O H C W N I A A Q S U
O U A E C N I P I E I M A D
P A I S S E L L E L N U B E
F S P U D N E T N E L A M F T L R
```

These stories continue at
www.French-Word-A-Day.com.